SMALL
CHURCH ON A

MISSION

JEFF ALLEN

SM🏠LL
CHURCH ON A
BIG
MISSION

Cultivating Missional Discipleship
in Smaller Churches

Small Church on a Big Mission
© Copyright 2017 by Jeff Allen

Printed in the United States of America

Design: Blake Berg

ISBN: 978-0-9990039-3-0

3DM Publishing
3dmpublishing.com

CONTENTS

Part Three: Purposeful Direction – Focus, Future, Function, and Formative Language

ACKNOWLEDGEMENTS

Praising God for the opportunity to live a life of adventure
as a disciple of Jesus Christ.

With thanks to Elyse, my forever girlfriend
as we live the adventure together.

ENDORSEMENT

Small church on a BIG Mission is a book that embodies its own message: it packs a BIG payoff into a small volume! Pastor, discipler, and missional leader Jeff Allen offers practical resources and proven strategies, drawing on his own experience of transitioning a smaller established church into a community of disciples who are living beyond themselves as a Family on Mission. Distilling many of the essential tools and vehicles developed by Mike Breen and 3DMovements, Allen shows how these can be applied to churches without large staffs, big budgets, and expansive facilities. If you are a leader of a smaller church and want to learn how to multiply disciples who are moving beyond the walls of your church to reach people in your community, then this book is for you!

Bob Rognlien
author of *Empowering Missional Disciples* and *A Jesus-Shaped Life*

FOREWORD

by Mike Breen

My first book published in 1991 was called *Growing the Smaller Church*, the publishers wanted a book that encouraged English clergy who were wrestling with the realities of leading smaller congregations. Now as then, the vast majority of congregations in Europe and the US are small and yet it is the pastors of the large congregations that get to write most of the books. But the small church has a vital – I would say indispensable role – in the mission of God, and so I was delighted to be asked to write the forward to Jeff Allen's new book. *Small Church on a Big Mission* is an excellent place for any leader of a typical sized church to begin considering the issues of discipleship and mission. This book will help you far more than the books written by mega church pastors operating in contexts that are so unlike your own they may as well be describing mission on a different planet!

We have all marveled at the television programs that document the vast variety of ecosystems on our planet. Like the biosphere the world of human culture is vast and infinitely varied and if we only had big churches we would find it difficult to relate to these multiplicities. But small churches can embed in the cracks and crevices of our culture and reach the multitudes of different groups and subcultures found within it. If our call, as the Great Commission suggests, is to reach every people group, then we need small churches that can identify with these people groups and share the gospel with them in contextually relevant ways, the broad-brush strokes of mega-church messaging will simply not suffice.

But don't get me wrong *Small Church on a Big Mission* is not a study in mega church bashing – no one wants to do that. There are two very clear paths in the future development of the American church, one leads to mega the other leads to micro church and both are absolutely essential. We will continue to need churches that are contextualized to the mass-market consumer culture of North America, able to communicate in broad gospel categories to large swathes of the population. But at the same time we will need churches that can operate in the smaller ecosystems of the nation's subcultures.

To a discouraged group of returned exiles struggling to rebuild the Temple in Jerusalem Zechariah said 'who despises the day of small things?' small things are important to God and so should never be despised by any of us. You may feel that your work is the aptly described as 'the day of small things' but in this book you will find no lament or critique, only hope, opportunity and celebration. Your work is not insignificant, on the contrary, your church like all the small churches in America present an enormous prospect for God's mission to our nation. As urban and rural communities become more fissile and liable to form smaller units of culture the Lord will sharpen these precise tools of missional engagement to do great things in our world. My prayer is that as you read this book you and your congregation will be sharpened to do the work you are uniquely called to do.

INTRODUCTION

This book celebrates the blessing of being a part of a small church on a BIG Mission. While we often read and hear stories of the big companies and larger churches in our communities, statistics reflect that the significant majority of businesses (99 percent in fact) and churches are small.

Perhaps there is something to be said for the blessing of being small that our culture often chooses to ignore. For such a time as this, in the midst of a rapidly changing context of church and ministry, I am blessed to serve as a pastor of a relatively small church that happens to be a part of one of the mainline denominational groups (Reformed Church in America). The journey of being pastor has been far from easy (as the following chapters confess), yet it has also been a journey filled with blessings that I could never have imagined decades ago—blessings that have helped me celebrate that I am a part of a small church on a Big Mission.

This book is basically a journal of discovery. It chronicles my discovery of who I am as a beloved child of God and reflects the character and competences that God has been developing in me over the last fifteen-plus years through a variety of ministry experiences. Most importantly, this book communicates a host of reflections on the call of discipleship and mission that God has placed on my life. This journey of discovery has led me to celebrate the blessings of being small while engaging in the Big Mission of revealing the Kingdom of God.

At the outset, let me share a bit of my story. The journey toward ministry and to Faith Community Church has been a long and winding road.

After spending nearly two decades in sales & marketing and training with various Fortune 100 companies, I was urged by my wife and others to follow a call to ministry that I had sensed during my college years. The transition from business to seminary and then eventually to vocational ministry was a significant shift in culture, to say the least. It took eight total years (first taking night classes and then part-time classes while serving on staff at Trinity Reformed Church in Holland, Michigan). Eventually the Graduation March played, and our family was on its way to Colorado.

I specifically recall one seminary course. During the first several weeks of class, the discussion addressed the question of whether the topic of leadership was relevant in the church. While some folks stated that leadership and specifically that talk of the gift of leadership can be overemphasized, my perception is that Jesus provided a living example of servant leadership that was intentional and that was viewable, doable, and reproducible by his disciples. Paul's encouragement to live a life worthy of imitation also strongly speaks of the importance of servant leadership for us both as disciples and as leaders in the church.

While this book is not specifically focused on leadership, it includes references that speak of my journey of personal transformation and my growing understanding of what it looks like to be a servant leader. My hope is that these references will help you consider your personal journey of discovery while also helping you to consider enduring truths of leadership that hold constant regardless of context or circumstance.

THE FOCUS OF THE BOOK

If you are looking for a resource that will provide you with a "let's grow the church fast" strategy or provide you with the next program to inspire your church forward, this is probably not the resource for you.

If, however, you are looking for practical principles for moving and shaping your culture toward discipleship and mission that celebrate the bigness of God's Kingdom, then this book is definitely for you.

THE STRUCTURE OF THE BOOK

This book is a journal of discovery sharing practical principles of discipleship and mission personally applied as a disciple and leader within a small church on a Big Mission.

This book is divided into three sections reflecting my journey of *Personal Transformation*, the *Practical Realities* encountered along the journey that many have asked me to share, and the *Purposeful Direction* undertaken together with other leaders in our context as a small church on a Big Mission.

Each chapter begins with a *story* from my journal of discovery followed by helpful *resources and tools* that have been applied in this topic. Each chapter concludes with a few questions for personal *reflection and discovery* as you consider taking steps in your own context.

PART 1

PERSONAL TRANSFORMATION
MY JOURNEY AS A DISCIPLE AND LEADER

1
SMALL CHURCH ON A BIG MISSION
Living out Discipleship and Mission

I know what it is to be in need, and I know what it is to have plenty. I have learned the secret of being content in any and every situation, whether well fed or hungry, whether living in plenty or in want. I can do all this through him who gives me strength.
—Philippians 4:12-13

STORY

It was early in the fall of 2012. School was about to start, and the schedule was ramping up for the launch of church programs. My wife and I had just come off a time of much-needed sabbatical after seven years of ministry in Littleton, Colorado. We returned rested, albeit with a bit of hesitancy at what was before us during the journey ahead.

To be completely honest, we had embarked on the sabbatical and spent the first six weeks simply recovering from a very long and challenging season of leading the church. During our first few years in Littleton, the church experienced back-to-back seasons of growth, capital improvement, and the launching of a second worship service seeking to attract a new demographic to the church. These efforts were on target with our mission and vision and were intended to move us forward on a trajectory of growth of the Kingdom of God. While this was the intended direction, and while the efforts initially moved the church in this direction, after a few years the church then experienced challenging back-to-back seasons of conflict and decline culminating in the ending of the second worship service launched years before.

A few months prior to the sabbatical, I had attended a Discipleship and Mission Workshop sponsored by 3DM. During the workshop my heart was struck by the statement that *"If you build the church, sometimes you get disciples. When you make disciples, you always get the church."* While many other teachings were shared during the workshop, this phrase hit me and drew me back in time to the countless conversations shared with my wife and others about my calling to vocational ministry years before.

Returning from the sabbatical in the late summer of 2012, I was greeted with a host of challenges ranging from worship attendance to personal conflicts that had gone unresolved during my time away. As together we sorted through the opportunities and challenges, I recognized that the Holy Spirit was stirring something in me through the challenge shared by Mike Breen during the Discipleship & Mission workshop months earlier. I was being invited into a new season of deep personal transformation. I strongly sensed that I was supposed to be in Littleton, CO for just such a time as this.

Perhaps more importantly, I was sensing that I was no longer going to simply do or play church. Rather, the Holy Spirit was clarifying my calling to be a disciple who makes disciples as a part of a small church on a Big Mission.

RESOURCES AND TOOLS

At this point in each chapter, I will share a few resources that have been particularly helpful and practical in my personal journey and in the collective journey of our church family. Since my journey of discovery has taken place both in the church and the business world, various leadership resources are included.

In *The Truth about Leadership: The No-fads, Heart-of-the-Matter Facts You Need to Know*, Jim Kouzes and Barry Posner suggest that one of the truths of leadership is that challenge is the crucible for greatness (page 91). Challenge was a place I knew all too well. This is what I was feeling after returning from sabbatical, and in truth the crucible was where I felt I had been for many years prior to the sabbatical. In the family system of churches, I knew all too well that challenging the status quo was not a comfortable place to be. As stated earlier, while the first few seasons in Littleton went well, the last several seasons had brought pain and challenge in abundance.

In our context, the church leadership was sensing challenge in the areas of discipleship and leadership. After many hours and weeks of discussion, we acknowledged that while the church was generally willing to listen to the counsel and teaching of the pastor, the leadership collectively needed to step up and follow Jesus Christ as the Head of the Church. Moreover, the leaders needed to personally step up in response to Jesus' challenge provided in the great commission to go and make disciples.

We completed our third church assessment in twelve years, and for all practical purposes we were considered to be a resourcing congregation. While so much about our church was good and healthy, there was one underlying element lying beneath the surface that we needed to dig deep to uncover. Assessing our situation and the many questions of the assessment, the board named the challenge that we were facing in the church as a heart condition.

We had been diagnosed with a heart condition! As you can imagine, this took a bit of processing on the part of our board and leadership group as we considered the root causes and possible treatments that would help us to heal as well as to live out the mission and vision given to us from the head.

As we considered the root causes of this problem and possible solutions, the leadership concluded that we needed to do four things:

- Address the strongholds in worship—Specifically, we needed to reboot worship to focus our gathered time as a family in the areas of:

    1. **Movement:** Opening our Heart for refinement, connection, and submission to the heart of God

    2. **Message:** Hearing truth from God's Word as we weekly consider: *What is God saying? and What am I going to do about it?*

    3. **Mission:** Applying the truth as we go out into the world to reflect the character and competencies of Jesus Christ

- Focus on personal transformation and disciple-making
- Live out the New Testament culture and be a "family on mission"
- Celebrate that we are small church on a Big Mission

CELEBRATING AS A SMALL CHURCH ON A BIG MISSION

Littleton has experienced a lot of demographic change over a relatively short period of time. Faith Community Church was planted in 1976 as a storefront ministry seeking to reach folks who might not go through the door of a traditional church (which was a pretty creative approach for its day). The Littleton area was rapidly growing, and so the church purchased property in an undeveloped area inhabited by prairie dogs not far from places referred to as Coal Mine, Jackass Hill, and the Ken Caryl Ranch. Faith was one of the first churches in the area along a dirt road that has since become a north-south highway connecting with the southwestern bypass of Denver. In an area where we were one of the first churches to pop up, today we are one of the smaller churches amongst many with several larger churches around us.

One day a frequent visitor shared how she often went with her husband to one of the larger churches in the area. While she celebrated their many opportunities and spectacular musical dramas during the holiday season, she said that she loved coming to our little church because it felt like family.

Her comment stuck with me and has become our position statement. Simply, we are a small church on a Big Mission. During the post-sabbatical season of ministry, our board began to recognize and to live into the reality that a lot of things all around us were changing. Yet in the midst of this change, Jesus was inviting (perhaps calling) us to be who God had made us to be and to live in the Kingdom of God as a small church on a Big Mission. We were being invited to grow where we were planted and to live out the Kingdom of God in our context making disciples who make disciples.

Over the coming months the board reflected, prayed, and shed tears. We together moved through denial, anger, bargaining, and depression to eventually accept the truth that the approaching season of adaptive change was necessary and that it would undoubtedly lead our small church to look and live differently. We acknowledged that moving to a disciple-making culture might prompt more people to leave and that budgets might get tight. Furthermore, as we obediently followed God's call, we knew that other unforeseen challenges might arise that we couldn't even begin to imagine.

Change Sucks

I celebrate that our board and staff leaned forward into this new challenging season embarking together on this journey toward discipleship and mission. We recognize that we have made a lot of mistakes and have learned much along the way. With humility, we celebrate that all that has occurred that reveals the Kingdom goes solely to the glory of God.

As a leader, I also accept the responsibility that much of what has not gone well is most likely a result of the shortcomings in my character and competency. I thank God for his grace and mercy in the midst of the journey. While I acknowledge my shortcomings, I also take comfort that the blood of Christ… cleanses our consciences from acts that lead to death (Hebrews 9:14; I Peter 3:21). I praise God for the great many emerging saints that I have been blessed to journey with at Faith Community Church.

As a part of this journey, we have been blessed to grow by practicing using the resources and tools of 3DMovement and from Mike Breen. In addition to the Mission Workshop experienced in January 2012, I was blessed to be in a coaching Huddle as well as to journey with 3DM practitioners in a two-year Learning Community. Many of the resources shared in this book were experienced as a part of my Learning Community experience with Dave Cheadle, Craig Broek, Peter Holwerda, and a host of others in the Denver area utilizing the tools and resources of 3DM.

REFLECTION AND DISCOVERY
Questions for application in your context

1. What are your reflections on Mike Breen's challenge that "when you build the church, sometimes you get disciples, but when you make disciples you always get the church"?

2. In your context, what are the challenges that you have tended to ignore, work around, or push to the side and avoid?

2
WHO AM I?
A Disciple Called to Make Missional Disciples

*Then Jesus came to them and said, "All authority in heaven and on earth
has been given to me. Therefore go and make disciples of all nations,
baptizing them in the name of the Father and of the Son and of the Holy
Spirit, and teaching them to obey everything I have commanded you.
And surely I am with you always, to the very end of the age.*
—Matthew 28:18-20

STORY

For the first few years of church ministry, I read a host of books and
participated in several conferences focused on leadership. In hindsight, I
think that I bought into a lot of what was being said in these conferences
and their focus on growth, leadership, and mission and vision. I also
recognize that I somewhat selfishly enjoyed these conferences as they
were encouraging and tended to affirm me as a leader and the direction
we were going.

I recall sharing lunch with one of my seminary professors who was visiting
Colorado. As we talked about all that was going well, he said, "When
ministry is good, it is really good". He then added, "And when ministry
is bad, it is often really bad". While I nodded my head in agreement, I
knew I was presently riding the wave of one of those good times. What

I didn't know at that moment was that the not-so-good times were fast approaching like an unexpected tsunami.

A few years later I attended a conference in San Antonio with my wife that focused on leadership and the future of the church. Today, I can't recall the name of the conference or the insights shared by exemplary teachers. My recollection has nothing to do with the quality of the speakers or the ideas being shared. Rather, my poor memory was reflective of the new season in which I found myself. The situational context of ministry had changed radically, and I was now in one of those seasons of ministry that was unbearably bad. We were neck-deep in a season of adaptive change. The completed capital campaign focusing on facility upgrades and intentional outreach to the emerging generation had brought to the surface implicit values existing within the family system of our local church.

While the tactical elements of the capital improvement project had gone well, the proposed changes elevated anxiety within the family system. The tactical elements that created the most significant anxiety were not surprising. In fact, we thought as a leadership team that we were prepared to address them. A few of the most anxiety-producing improvements included:

- Upgrading the sound system and increasing the size of the stage area (which resulted in the replacement of a choir loft with choir risers)

- The installation of a stone cross and a waterfall along with an immersion baptismal tank that would serve as focal point in the worship center (replacing a wooden cross that previously hung on the wall behind the choir loft)

- The installation of new chairs replacing the pews (which would have cost three times as much money to refurbish).

While anxiety in the family system around these areas was anticipated and discussed at length in advance, we significantly underestimated the way folks would react and respond to these changes. While I personally anticipated some of these improvements to be challenging, I felt we had laid a foundation for change during the previous years through sermons and our focus on the values and the vision. I had naively thought that our family system was ready to embrace these adaptive changes and to move to the next level. I was wrong. I now realize that I was unconsciously incompetent—I didn't know what I didn't know.

Over time, a few surprising and highly inappropriate actions came to the surface from a few people in the church. While I navigated the challenging terrain as best I could, my own personal walk with Christ began to suffer and my heart became calloused because of the attacks being brought against me as the leader. In hindsight, I now understand that my character and competency needed to be developed in order to move forward with the vision and to regain the forward momentum we had been experiencing in the previous season of ministry. But at that time, I was living in the valley of the shadow of death.

By the time the San Antonio conference came around, I was completely fried as a disciple and leader. The seemingly never-ending coffee conversations and home meetings, coupled with the unsigned letters of accusation delivered from fictitious post office boxes, left me exhausted, angry, and more than a little bitter toward the church and God's people in general. I began to understand more clearly why Moses grumbled.

It took me years to recover physically, emotionally, and spiritually from those early years in ministry. I now understand why so many pastors don't stick around long after a capital campaign or for the most part don't stay at a church long enough to receive a sabbatical.

RESOURCES AND TOOLS

In general, I am an optimist about circumstances as well as about people and their motivations. I recall Hope College Professor Tony Muiderman sharing in a management class about the Theory X and Theory Y styles of management. Theory X assumes that people dislike work and that they want to avoid it and do not want to take responsibility. Theory Y, on the other hand, assumes that people are self-motivated and thrive on responsibility. I have always been a Theory Y kind of guy. This optimistic view toward people in general made me susceptible to the attacks of a few people in the church.

Reflecting on the challenging years in Littleton, I realize that my experiences with a few people significantly darkened my perspective of *all* people and my perception of their under-the-surface hidden motivations. A dark cloud had come on the horizon, and I felt like I was in a season of "Ridin' the Storm Out." (This is one of my favorite REO Speedwagon songs, and I recently learned was written while the band was touring in Colorado. Of course.)

During this season I began to feel that I was moving as a pastor toward being a part of the category of the "dones"—those believers who look at the way so-called Christians and churches behave and think "I want very little to do with it. I'm done." Why not? My experience had taught me first-hand how nasty so-called Christians can be.

A number of books and resources were helpful during these stormy years: *The Hole in our Gospel* by Richard Stearns, *The Prodigal God* and *Gospel in Life* by Timothy Keller, *Taking your Church to the Next Level: What Got You Here Won't Get You There* by Gary L. McIntosh to name a few. These books helped me see a bit of my journey in the journey of others while also casting a vision for UP, IN, and OUT development.

During one of my darkest night of the soul seasons, *Unexplainable: Pursuing a Life Only God can make Possible* by Don Cousins provided me with a glimpse of light needed in vocational ministry. In the section entitled *LifeShift 2—From Temporal to Eternal*, Cousins writes about faithfulness, fruitfulness, and the ultimate measure of success. This section helped me to understand some of the trials I was experiencing and the character that was being developed in me (page 112), while also pointing me toward what it could look to live a life worthy of imitation (page 143). In the midst of the valley of the shadow of death, I had a brief glimpse of light that my heart could fully embrace.

Building on this brief glimpse of light, the resources from 3DM and *Building a Discipling Culture* by Mike Breen significantly re-directed my life and journey as a disciple and equipping leader. While engaging in the Learning Community process over two years, I engaged in a disciple-making Huddle online with a coach in Fort Wayne, Indiana, by the name of Henry Graf. In many ways, Henry was a Barnabas-like encourager for me during a challenging time of learning. As I began applying the tools shared in *Building a Discipling Culture* to my journey as a disciple, the Holy Spirit began breaking down the calloused walls of self-protection that I had built up during the previous years of pain and challenge. In this new season, I began to understand more clearly the *message of Jesus* as I applied the *way of Jesus* to my life.

Questioning My Identity: As stated previously, over time my heart began to soften, and my passion for the kingdom of God began to grow. While I had always known and understood that I was a beloved child of God, the years of ministry challenge and pain had brought me to a point of thinking of myself as a failure. I was beginning to believe the lie of the enemy that I was a failure and that I was unworthy of the love of my heavenly father.

Encouragement in the Midst of the Valley: In this online coaching Huddle, I received relevant biblical teaching that was memorable and reproducible both in my life and in my church context. Though I was in a very dark period in the valley of the shadow, I was encouraged and reminded within the Huddle of Jesus' message and the *vision* that the time had come and that the Kingdom of Heaven has come near. In my questioning, I was given *grace* and permission to grieve and to share the pain I had experienced. And I was encouraged *time* and *time again* to reclaim my birthright as a child of God to hear the voice of my lovingly heavenly father.

Throughout my church life, I had always valued community and biblical accountability. In this new season within the vehicle of Huddle, I was experiencing, practicing, and beginning to live out *the word* of truth and grace as well as *the way* of truth and grace in a similar way that Jesus shared with his disciples.

Earlier I mentioned Timothy Keller's book *The Prodigal God*. My experience in Huddle began to reveal that in some ways my life mirrored the life of the elder brother in the New Testament story of the Prodigal Son. I was living my understanding of the covenant nature of God's love backward. I was seeking to earn my identity as a beloved child of my heavenly Father through obedient service.

Please, hear what I am saying: <u>I basically was living</u> out *<u>what I didn't believe</u>*. While I understood the nature of grace, I was living and working so hard that I was actually becoming bitter because I wasn't getting out of ministry what I thought was a fair return for my investment! I understood the nature of Covenant love, yet I was unintentionally living the Covenant love of God backward (as reflected in the following graphic): If I am obedient, I will earn my Father's love.

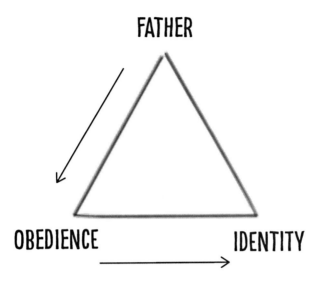

Instead of Faithfulness (as acknowledged by Don Cousins), I was hearing the voice of my Father and seeking to obediently earn my space as a beloved child of the King. My backward approach was short-circuiting God's love and the gift of grace. My backward approach was causing me pain, aggravation, and anxiety. I might add that it wasn't helpful to the folks I was ministering to either.

In the midst of Huddle, God, through the power of the Holy Spirit placed the truth of love and grace back in my heart that *I am a beloved child of God.* Over time, the arrows began to reverse directions. More and more I was living into the Covenant truth that *I am a beloved child of God.* As I did, I began to experience freedom from the expectations and pressures of others and began hearing God's voice with greater clarity as well as obediently following this voice from my heavenly Father.

Listening to the voice of the Father doesn't mean that I no longer care about others or even about what others might have to say. Rather it clarified and centered me in the truth within my heart that *I am a beloved child of God.* First and foremost I know that God desires the very best for me as one of his children. Therefore, while I invite and listen to the counsel of others, I have learned most importantly to listen to and to obey the voice of God.

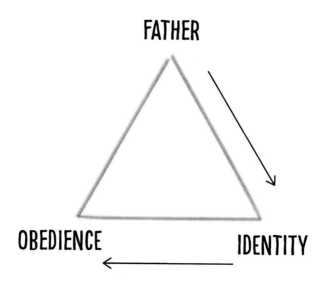

I celebrate that *I am a beloved child of God*. I celebrate that *I am a beloved disciple of the King*. Furthermore, I celebrate and obediently trust that *I am a beloved disciple who is called to make other disciples* as together we are living out the Kingdom of God on earth.

REFLECTION AND DISCOVERY
Questions for application in your context

1. *In practice, do you live each day in joyful obedience responding to the voice of our heavenly Father?*

    • *If so, share a relevant example from this past week of your joyful obedience to the Father's voice.*

    • *If not, share a current story of where you are struggling with obedience or with sensing the love of God in your life.*

2. *The concluding paragraph of this chapter suggests that we are beloved disciples who are called to make other disciples. Do you believe this to be true?*

    - *If so, with whom are you presently engaged in a disciple-making relationship?*
    - *If not, what are you going to do about it?*

3
WHAT IS GOD INVITING ME TO DO?
Being a Living Example Worthy of Imitation

*I am writing this not to shame you but to warn you as my dear children.
Even if you had ten thousand guardians in Christ, you do not have many
fathers, for in Christ Jesus I became your father through the gospel.
Therefore I urge you to imitate me.*
—1 Corinthians 4:14-16

STORY

The Senior Access Missional Community meets each Thursday morning for folks 55 and older. One day in the fall of 2015, we shared an interactive teaching time about the life and journey of the Apostle Paul. As a part of this UP time (seeking to shape our heart to be a reflection of the heart of our heavenly Father), we discussed Paul's first letter to the church in Corinth. Paul speaks about being servants of God and about those who judge his conduct, and he offers encouragement for the Corinthian church to seek out fathers in Christ through the gospel. Paul concludes his encouragement by lifting up a significant challenge in 4:16: "Therefore I urge you to imitate me. "

After a bit of discussion, I invited the folks gathered to talk in small groups around their tables about their living example and whether they would accept Paul's challenge of "urging others to imitate their life in Christ".

As we debriefed the discussion around the tables, one of the participants stated that Paul's statement could be considered a bit egotistical, and then added that he did not want others to imitate his living example. While I agreed that we always want to avoid being self-centered, egotistical, and self-promoting, I asserted that we also want to avoid false humility that gives us permission to deny the discipleship challenge that Paul is elevating in this passage from 1 Corinthians. In short, we, like the church in Corinth, need to step up as a part of journey of discipleship and live a life worthy of imitation.

RESOURCES AND TOOLS

Considering Paul's statement to the church at Corinth, our living example needs to be so strong that others look at the way we live and should be inspired to imitate our way of living.

This has perhaps been one of the most significant lessons impacting me as a disciple and leader in the Kingdom of God. While I celebrate much of the instruction received during my seminary years, the most helpful lessons have been received in life-on-life apprenticeship engaging with disciple-making leaders in the 3DM network.

Within the context of 3DM coaching Huddles and Missional Communities, I have experienced a grace-filled and challenging space to develop my *character* as a disciple of Jesus Christ while also receiving practical instruction and opportunities for developing *competencies* as disciple-maker on mission in the world.

I realized that Jesus did what so many of us hesitate to do. When Jesus was apprenticing the disciples, he not only shared *information* (the word), but also rather quickly sent them out two by two to *imitate* his living example (the way).

So what's my point? It is simply this: during the dark season of my journey in Littleton, I didn't have a lot of people coming up to me expressing a desire to imitate me. This was a *kairos* God breaking through time moment of significant proportion. This *kairos* moment required countless hours of reflection, prayer, discussion, pruning, and planning in my personal life and in my role as a pastor. If you are a pastor reading this, I invite you to ask yourself right now if folks are coming up to you asking questions and expressing a desire to imitate your living example. If not, then perhaps there is something God is trying to say to you in this moment as well.

The *kairos* moments prompted in me ranged from time management to my style of delivering sermons. The *kairos* moments prompted in our family ranged from having conversations with my bride about hosting a missional community in our home to hosting fire pit Fridays so we could provide folks being Huddled with greater access to our lives. The *kairos* moments have been so numerous that they look rather like a Slinky of circles in which one *kairos* has prompted another and then yet another *kairos*, all of them impacting my life and our life rhythms as a family.

I cannot emphasize enough the significance of coming to grips with Paul's challenge to live a life worthy of imitation. As I draw this chapter and section to a close, let me offer one more story. I have always been blessed to journey with older folks. I like them, and they tend to like me. I remember facilitating a Sunday School class several decades ago that included a wide range of ages and included a number of senior adults. While I cannot remember the topic of the day or the specific passages of scripture being discussed, I remember with clarity the statement that Theresa Hargterink made that Sunday morning so long ago. She said, "Your life may be the only Bible that some folks will ever read." She understood Paul's challenge to live a life worthy of imitation.

I celebrate the countless Holy Spirit-directed changes occurring in my life and the new rhythm being lived out as a disciple of Jesus Christ. Praise God from whom all blessings flow! In this new season, there are a seemingly ever-increasing number of folks that God is bringing into the orbit of our family and our small church on a Big Mission.

I celebrate that God is providing in this harvest season, and I invite you to join me in living a life worthy of imitation.

REFLECTION AND DISCOVERY
Questions for application in your context

1. *The Apostle Paul challenges the Church in Corinth to "imitate me." What would need to change in your life in order for you to publicly urge others to imitate you?*

2. *Finally, as a disciple of Jesus Christ, are folks coming up to you and asking what it is that makes your living example different from others in our culture?*

    • *If not, please reflect on why you sense folks are not coming to you in this way.*

    • *If so, what do you think they see that is prompting them to imitate you?*

PART 2

PRACTICAL REALITIES

**POSITION, POWER, PRUNING, POLITY,
PARTNERING, AND PIPELINE**

4
POSITION
Recognizing Where I Am in My Journey

Come to me, all you who are weary and burdened, and I will give you rest. Take my yoke upon you and learn from me, for I am gentle and humble in heart, and you will find rest for your souls. For my yoke is easy and my burden is light.
—Matthew 11:28-30

STORY

The last several years have taught me the importance of being both a sheep and a shepherd. Just as the disciples were led and taught by Jesus as they walked along the road, they also were sent out to usher in the Kingdom of God. Ultimately, the disciples were sent out to make disciples of all nations (Matthew 28:18) and were reminded and encouraged that as they went "they will do even greater things" (John 14:12).

SHEEPHERD

In my personal journey as a disciple and as a disciple-making leader, there were countless occasions when I took the time to stop and assess my current position in my journey as a disciple of Jesus Christ.

While I have taken a number of assessments during my business years, one of the most significant assessments in the church context took place when I was a student at Western Theological Seminary. Professor Matt Floding invited the students in our Formation for Ministry seminar to complete a brief personal assessment by answering 24 questions. The responses were grouped into eight discipleship dimensions that ranged from Trust in God's saving grace and believes firmly in the humanity and divinity of Jesus to Serves humanity consistently, and passionately through acts of love and justice. In addition to assessing the eight discipleship dimensions, the responses could also be summarized into two overall themes of:

1) A person of mature faith experiences both a life-transforming relationship to a loving God (vertical theme)

2) A consistent devotion to serving others (horizontal theme)

The results were then plotted on a grid like this:

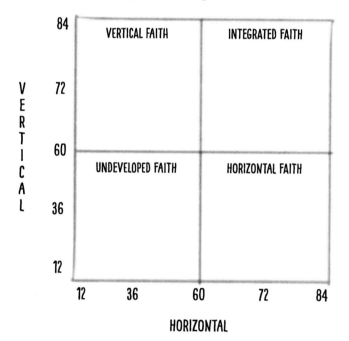

When I completed the assessment, I was a bit surprised to realize that while I scored pretty well on the vertical theme of mature faith, I was definitely lacking in the horizontal theme of devotedly serving others.

This assessment told me that I had some growing to do as a disciple of Jesus Christ. In my particular case, the growth previously emphasized knowledge and learning without much application. Today I would state it this way: my growth had been focused on information and needed to move into imitation. The assessment affirmed I was doing pretty well in the UP dimension, but I needed some work in the OUT dimension. I needed to put my beliefs into action in more consistent and practical ways.

RESOURCES AND TOOLS

Over the years, I took a few more discipleship assessments (like the one offered by Randy Frazee in the *Connecting Church: Beyond Small Groups to Authentic Community*) and encouraged others through the Sunday School classes I taught at the church to do the same.

I noticed that while folks will take countless assessments for growth and development in their workplace, these same people tend to hesitate when it comes to taking assessments regarding their journey of discipleship. Some of this hesitancy might come from the perception that my discipleship journey is private. Another possibility could be that we have effectively trained people in the church about what assessments entail. For example, when gift assessments are offered, the final part of the course is usually a meeting with the Connection Leader in order to "plug" the person into a place of service inside the church. While this can be affirming and encouraging for a congregant, it can also be perceived as a way for the church to feed the machine by plugging people into empty places that are needed to keep the institution running.

At Faith Community Church, we wanted to provide disciples with a discipleship self-assessment that they could complete entirely on their own. While we offered to provide assistance, the primary outcome of the self-assessment was for folks to be able to see a picture of where they were at in their personal journey of discipleship and to help them identify their next steps. The purpose of the assessment was to identify their current position as a disciple of Jesus Christ and then to help them develop their own plans for moving forward as God directed.

Using the assessment experienced in seminary as a guide, we applied a bit of innovation creating a discipleship self-assessment using the *character (being like Jesus)* and *competency (doing the things that Jesus did)* questions provided in the appendix of Mike Breen's book *Building a Discipling Culture*. The character and competency questions invite disciples to assess where they are in three dimensions that Jesus demonstrated in his life and ministry: UP, IN, & OUT.

Luke 6:12-19 clearly shows the three-dimensional shape of Jesus' life and ministry.

- **UP dimension:** [12]One of those days Jesus went out to a mountainside to pray, and spent the night praying to God.

- **IN dimension:** [13]When morning came, he called his disciples to him and chose twelve of them, whom he also designated apostles: [14]Simon (whom he named Peter), his brother Andrew, James, John, Philip, Bartholomew, [15]Matthew, Thomas, James son of Alpheus, Simon who was called the Zealot, [16]Judas son of James, and Judas Iscariot, who became a traitor.

- **OUT dimension:** [17]He went down with them and stood on a level place. A large crowd of his disciples was there and a great number of people from all over Judea, from Jerusalem, and from the coastal region around Tyre and Sidon, [18]who had come to hear him and to be healed of their diseases. Those troubled by impure spirits were cured, [19]and the people all tried to touch him, because power was coming from him and healing them all.

At Faith Community Church, we often speak about the three-dimensional life of a disciple using the words Reflection, Relationships, and Responsibility. We also use the below as a picture of what the Jesus shaped life of a disciple looks like.

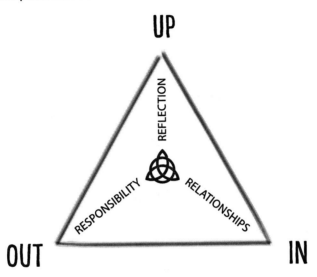

Being +
Doing

UP / REFLECTION—To what extent does my character *reflect* the *good* character of Jesus Christ? And to what extent does my time and energy *reflect* the competencies or the skills that Jesus taught and demonstrated in his walk with his disciples?

IN / RELATIONSHIPS—To what extent do I develop and engage in *relationships* that develop in others the character that Jesus developed with his disciples? And to what extent do my *relationships* demonstrate the competency and skills that Jesus demonstrated with his disciples?

OUT / RESPONSIBILITY—To what extent does my character move me to engage and live out the *responsibility* that Jesus gave his disciples to be his witnesses to their Jerusalem, Judea, Samaria, and to the ends of the earth? To what extent do I effectively demonstrate this competency and skill as I engage this *responsibility*?

As people take the self-assessment, we remind them that the purpose of this *Three-Dimensional Discipleship Self-Assessment Tool* is to provide a snapshot of where they are at this moment in time. As we journey together in our lifelong process of transformation, we pray that this *discipleship assessment tool* is helpful in identifying and planning areas of growth for their continuing journey as a disciple of Jesus Christ.

As folks complete the self-assessment, they are invited to tabulate and plot their scores (see the triangle below) to reveal the shape of their personal discipleship triangle.

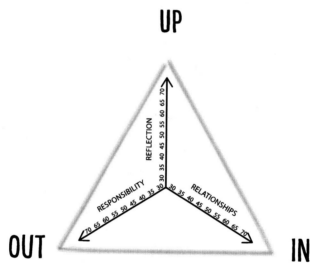

With their personal discipleship triangle revealed, people can reflect and discuss with others the character and competency questions where they scored the lowest as they develop a plan for their continuing journey as a disciple of Jesus Christ. Moving forward, the focus is to grow, to develop, and to mature as a more balanced three-dimensional disciple imitating the shape and the life of Jesus Christ.

We've included this assessment in Appendix #1 of this book. An online version of this assessment is also be available at www.smallchurchbigmission.org

My Personal Triangle as a Disciple

In my seminary years, I realized I had some work to do in demonstrating my beliefs by reaching out. When I completed the Three-Dimensional Disciple Self-Assessment, I realized that even though I was serving as a pastor in the church, I still had some OUT work to do. It made me realize that I was doing so much UP and IN with church people that I had little time or energy to go OUT. This is what my triangle looked like in 2013:

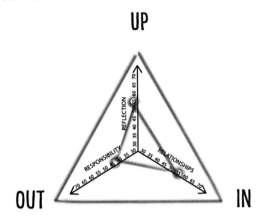

As I have completed of this self-assessment and developed corresponding plans over multiple years, it is amazing to see how God has re-shaped and transformed my heart as well as the work of my hands and feet. Here are the shapes of my triangles for 2014 and 2015:

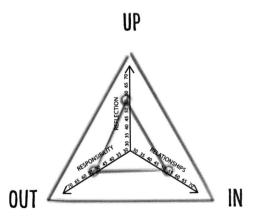

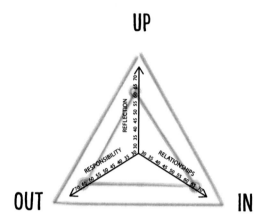

Three-Dimensional Disciple Assessments with the Staff & Board

In addition to using this assessment personally, you can also utilize it to paint a picture of the collective shape of a staff, a church board, or even an entire congregation.

Here's an example of the combined shape of our church board (called a Consistory) and a statistically significant sample of our whole church over the course of three years.

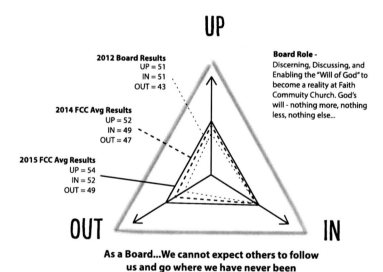

As a Board...We cannot expect others to follow us and go where we have never been

The triangles above elevate a couple of interesting observations and reflections:

- Observation #1: The triangle shape of the board and even the shape of the church as a whole was not too different than my personal triangle as pastor.

- Reflection #1: As a Board and as leaders in the church, we cannot expect others to follow us going to where we have never been. We have to lead by example, learning and living as a three-dimensional disciple who is worthy of imitation.

- Observation #2: The triangle shape of a person, of a board, and of a church is not static and changes over time.

- Reflection #2: Over the years as I put personal plans into action and as the staff and board implemented corresponding plans, the shape of our combined triangle as a church changed and began to better demonstrate the shape of Jesus' life of UP, IN, and OUT.

In closing let me encourage you to faithfully consider the position where you are at as a disciple of Jesus Christ. God loves you so much that he accepts you just the way you are. God knows exactly where you are at this moment as a disciple of Jesus Christ. As leaders in Christ's church, we cannot expect others to follow us and go to a place where we have never been before. So take the first step and recognize what is – what is the shape of your discipleship triangle? Next, begin to consider what could be as you move forward with faithful steps into the future.

REFLECTION AND DISCOVERY
Questions for application in your context

1. *Do you know where you are as a disciple of Jesus Christ? Specifically, can you share your plan for development and growth in the under-developed areas of your discipleship triangle?*

2.   *Read Matthew 11:28-30. Would others look at your life and affirm that in your living example, you have taken on the yoke to learn from Jesus?*

5
POWER
Relying on the Holy Spirit

On one occasion, while he was eating with them, he gave them this
command: "Do not leave Jerusalem, but wait for the gift my Father
promised, which you have heard me speak about.
—Acts 1:4

STORY

The early years of leading in the church were more than a bit challenging, to say the least. I hit a point (multiple times, actually) when I literally threw up my hands and cried aloud, "I cannot do this!" I now realize in hindsight that this was exactly the point. In the work of the church and of the kingdom, I can do nothing of kingdom significance in my own power.

Exodus 23:20-22 states, "See, I am sending an angel ahead of you to guard you along the way and to bring you to the place I have prepared. Pay attention to him and listen to what he says… if you listen carefully to what he says and do all that I say, I will be an enemy to your enemies and will oppose those who oppose you."

Many of us are quick to hold onto these encouraging words of instruction.

But the message doesn't stop there—verse 29 states: "But I will not drive them out in a single year, because the land would become desolate and the wild animals too numerous for you. Little by little I will drive them out before you, until you have increased enough to take possession of the land."

In these additional words, I recognize the reality that I am on a journey of transformation in which we increase little by little until we have increased enough to take possession of the territory that God is preparing for us in advance.

As we increase, we are not increasing in our own power. Rather, much like the apostle Paul's reflections in 2 Corinthians 11:30, our increase is an ever-growing increase of humility in which we state, "if I must boast, I will boast of the things that show my weakness."

In seminary we were encouraged to find our voice as we preached and proclaimed the word of God to the people. After more than 15 years, I sense that the voice of God is best heard through me when I simply share the message as if it is a conversation amongst disciples as we journey together through the text. While I prepare the message throughout the week (striving to have the main points of the message completed before noon on Thursday), the text continues to work on me the rest of the week until the message comes out on Sunday morning. I often find that the text and the message take on a life of its own by the time Sunday morning comes. Often (I could even say always), the message comes out of my mouth differently than I expected, as the text breathes and speaks into our Sunday morning gathering of the extended family on mission. This is one small example of how I have grown and am continuing to grow as I humble my intellectual capital and capacity to the leading of the Holy Spirit, inviting the spiritual capital of the kingdom of significantly greater value to speak and to direct our path.

RESOURCES AND TOOLS

The last ten years have provided countless opportunities for me to increase little by little, to learn, and to lean into the authority of the King and power of the Holy Spirit. These lessons are continuing daily. While countless stories could be told, in brief let me reflect upon the impact of my understanding of *oikonomics*, or said another way, the way the household (*oikos*) invests its time, energy, and resources in developing the Kingdom of God on earth.

In the book *Oikonomics* by Mike Breen and Ben Sternke, the five capitals that build the kingdom of God could be summarized as follows:

1. **Spiritual:** How much faith do you have to invest?
   Currency: Wisdom & Power

2. **Relational:** How much relational equity do you have to invest?
   Currency: Family & Friends

3. **Physical:** How much time and energy do you have to invest?
   Currency: Hours & Health

4. **Intellectual:** What intellect, skill sets, and competencies do you have to invest?
   Currency: Concepts & Ideas

5. **Financial:** How much financial capital do you have to invest?
   Currency: Dollars & Cents

You will notice that these capitals of the Kingdom are in order with the most valuable (Spiritual) listed at the top with the other capitals of the Kingdom listed in descending order. Not only are they listed in descending order, even more significant is the realization that each of the higher capitals is something like 10 times more important or valuable for the development of the kingdom than the one beneath it.

You probably have questions about this idea, and I'd encourage you to read the book to learn more. For now, let's focus on a salient point: our culture at large, as well as our church culture, tends to focus most on the capitals listed third, fourth, and fifth on the list above. We usually refer to these on Stewardship Sunday and throughout the year as *Time, Talent, and Treasure.*

While we often put the emphasis on these three capitals, Jesus' teaching emphasized spiritual and relational capital. In Matthew 13:44-46:

> *"The kingdom of heaven is like treasure hidden in a field. When a man found it, he hid it again, and then in his joy went and sold all he had and bought that field.*
>
> *Again, the kingdom of heaven is like a merchant looking for fine pearls."*

When he found one of great value, he went away and sold everything he had and bought it.

In short, the Kingdom of God is so greatly treasured that it completely blows away the value of *everything* else.

This point is further developed as Jesus speaks with the rich young man in Matthew 19:16-25:

> *"If you want to be perfect, go, sell your possessions and give to the poor, and you will have treasure in heaven. Then come, follow me."*

When the young man heard this, he went away sad, because he had great wealth.

Jesus was telling the potential disciple that the way you value capital in your life is completely backward. Spiritual capital is way more important than all of the other forms of capital. In fact, Jesus challenges the rich young man to get rid of it all and then come, follow me!

Jesus is not only speaking about Financial and Spiritual Capital—he is inviting the young man to invest Relational Capital and to join him in the journey of a lifetime—a journey in which all of the capitals of the Kingdom come into play. In this text, the rich young man passes up the opportunity of a lifetime in which relational capital could have been invested walking alongside Jesus as a disciple. This is clearly an example when the perceived value of one of the capitals (financial) impeded the development of other capital (relational and spiritual) of significantly greater value for building the Kingdom.

While significantly more can be said, let me close by reflecting on the life of the Apostle Paul. In the book of Acts, we see the journey of a disciple of Jesus who also is increasing little by little. By the time we reach chapter 16, we see a disciple who is now acting out his calling as an Apostle—one sent by Jesus.

In Acts 16:1-10, we see Paul doing what on one hand seems strange as he chose not to follow the permission given in the letter he carries from the Jerusalem Council and instead circumcises Timothy. On the other hand, Paul demonstrated his perseverance and astounding ability to stick to a plan as a Hebrew of Hebrews, and as to the law—a Pharisee. Paul is like a bloodhound in the sense that once he set his mind to something (like persecuting the believers in his earlier years as Saul), he generally sticks to the plan faultlessly. Yet in verses 4-10 of chapter 16, Paul is willing at a moments notice to drop his plan and to follow the vision of the man from

Macedonia who is begging him to "come over to Macedonia and help us." Verse 10 states, "After Paul had seen the vision, we got ready at once to leave for Macedonia, concluding that God had called us to preach the gospel to them."

While on the one hand Paul chooses to not follow the new instructions of the church and chooses to circumcise Timothy, on the other hand he abandons his plan on a moment's notice to follow a vision he receives in the night. In light of Paul's decade long journey as a disciple of Jesus Christ, what seems to be Paul going in two different directions is really more of a picture of Paul working hand in hand with God and Jesus as he follows the leading of the Holy Spirit.

In both cases Paul demonstrates the maturity and experience of a disciple-making leader who has journeyed many miles along the road. As it relates to Timothy, Paul knows all to well that Timothy's first stop in his missionary journeys will likely be the synagogue. This is a place where Paul spent a lot of time in his early years, and the words uttered to Ananias "that I will show him how much he must suffer" have literally been written in stripes on Paul's back. The wise and discerning leader we see in Acts 16 chooses to forego the letter of permission in his pocket and circumcises Timothy so that the only possible barrier for Timothy to overcome is that some may not accept him because of his youth.

As Paul follows the vision of Macedonia, Paul demonstrates how he has learned humility as he lays aside his thoughts and plans to follow the direction and leading of the Holy Spirit. From the moment he experiences Jesus and is struck blind on the road to Damascus in Acts 9, he begins a journey in which his vision and direction is increasingly clarified. By the time we reach Acts 16, Paul has cultivated a relationship with Jesus where he willingly submits to the direction and leading of God. It's a relationship in which Paul acknowledges and demonstrates through his living example that God's power is made perfect in my weakness.

I celebrate that God, through the power of the Holy Spirit, is revealing more and more of the Kingdom of Heaven on earth in our midst. As we value and lean into the excessively greater worth of Relational and Spiritual capital, God is demonstrated in a way that can only humble us as servants while we celebrate and offer glory to God.

REFLECTION AND DISCOVERY
Questions for application in your context

1. Look at the provided list of the Five Capitals of the Kingdom shared in this chapter. As you look at this list, reflect and place the Five Capitals in order according to the way you tend to value them and live your life:

    1 _____ *(most valuable)*

    2 _____

    3 _____

    4 _____

    5 _____ *(least valuable in terms of the others)*

2. Take time to pray the Lord's Prayer, placing particular emphasis on petition #6, which invokes the Father's power and deliverance over the schemes of the evil one. After you have prayed this prayer focusing on the King's power, what observations come to mind for you and your ministry? *Not my power to deliver, but Gods. Do I trust God?*

6
PRUNING
Releasing Areas of Distraction

I am the true vine, and my Father is the gardener. He cuts off every branch in me that bears no fruit, while every branch that does bear fruit he prunes so that it will be even more fruitful. You are already clean because of the word I have spoken to you. Remain in me, as I also remain in you. No branch can bear fruit by itself; it must remain in the vine. Neither can you bear fruit unless you remain in me. "I am the vine; you are the branches. If you remain in me and I in you, you will bear much fruit; apart from me you can do nothing. If you do not remain in me, you are like a branch that is thrown away and withers; such branches are picked up, thrown into the fire and burned. If you remain in me and my words remain in you, ask whatever you wish, and it will be done for you. This is to my Father's glory, that you bear much fruit, showing yourselves to be my disciples.
—John 15:1-8

STORY

If you are a pastor or serve on a church staff, you undoubtedly receive a constant stream of requests, ideas, and suggestions about things to do in the ministry. Many of these opportunities fall into the category of good things to do. The big question is how you discern the *good things* from the *God things*. More directly to the point, how do you prune some of the good things out of your schedule in order to make more room for the God things to grow and bear fruit?

A few years in to my ministry time in Littleton, we were blessed with the opportunity of doing a capital campaign. We did our due diligence and even brought in a fundraising consultant to help us with the process and to clearly articulate our priorities for the *Faith Forward* campaign. As the campaign came together, we articulated again and again that in moving *Faith Forward*, we were simply *Stepping UP living into our responsibility of Facility Stewardship, Disciple-making, and Church Planting*.

It was during this season that I learned that I couldn't burn the candle at both ends. Well, you can—but it comes at a significant price. In listening to the counsel of the fundraising consultant, many on our team stepped up to some seriously unhealthy rhythms in the forms of unending town meetings, home meetings, small group conversations, and the like. At the conclusion of the campaign, for a host of reasons (well beyond the number of meetings that took place), I along with a number of key leaders from the staff found themselves in a place of total and complete burnout.

Sharing stories with other pastors, I learned that it is quite common for a pastor to move on to another call within a few years following a significant fundraising campaign. I can now understand why this happens.

On the other end of the spectrum, during the summer of 2015 Faith Community Church conducted another fundraising campaign in support of its emerging partnership with *APEX Church* (a church plant with a sister denomination that was supported and invited to share worship space onsite with us). Because of our experience from years earlier, coupled with a deeper understanding of the Rhythm of Life demonstrated in scripture, we approached this new campaign and related construction with a much healthier perspective. When the campaign concluded, celebration was evident not only for the funds and facility upgrades delivered but most especially for the blessing of relational and spiritual capital developed while seeking financial capital in this season.

RESOURCES AND TOOLS

Pruning is hard and often painful work. When I first entered the 3DM disciple-making vehicle of Huddle, I thought my focus would primarily be on learning the information. After about the fifth or sixth Huddle session, the information and teaching of the Circle and Semi-Circle *LifeShapes* started a change within me. I realized that God had been saying a host of things (for a long while) that I wasn't particularly paying attention to. Over the course of several months and years, I started applying the *LifeShapes* to my own journey and began to move from simply having the Information toward living a life worthy of Imitation. This involved a lot of processing, prioritizing, and pruning.

As I reflect on the differences between the earlier campaign and the campaign of the summer 2015, the most significant difference had to do with my understanding and application of the Semi-Circle.

THE SEMI-CIRCLE

Genesis 1:26-2:3 Genesis 2:15 Genesis 3:8-9

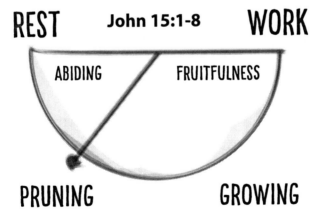

In the very beginning, we recognize that God established a rhythm of work and rest. God rested on the seventh day not because of being tired, but rather to help us to understand that this is part of the healthy rhythm of life. This rhythm is amplified and given significant clarity in Jesus' teaching in John 15:1-8 as we see how moving intentionally from rest to work with appropriate times of pruning will enable greater growth and fruit in the Kingdom.

During the capital campaign conducted in my early years in Littleton, many of us over-extended ourselves. The result was a crash that required an extended season of rest. In many ways, this season of rest or of laying fallow was unexpected, but it was necessary as we recuperated from the enormous expenditure of intellectual and physical capital during this campaign. Because we had over-extended ourselves so far, this season of rest and recuperation lasted many years.

By summer 2015, a significant amount of pruning of good things had taken place in my life, and in my daily, weekly, and seasonal rhythms. This pruning allowed the opportunity for new shoots to begin to grow in this new season. By this time, I was healthier and stronger in a variety of ways. As we moved into this new season, with the Semi-Circle in mind, we designed a different kind of capital campaign that was lightweight and low maintenance that shared the load of communication and construction in more healthy and God-honoring ways.

What's my point? The practical reality is that there is most likely some pruning that needs to be done in your schedule and in you as a disciple of Jesus Christ. This, by the way, is one of the things that the Three Dimensional Discipleship Assessment will help to uncover. Once you see the opportunities that God is saying to you, the important question becomes what are you going to do about it.

Often, the "What am I going to do about it" question is challenging. After all there are so many good things in your calendar each day and throughout the week. Where do you begin to prune?

> There is a time for everything, and a season for every activity under the heavens.
>
> —Ecclesiastes 3:1

I encourage us to go to Scripture and remember that for everything there is a time and a season under the heavens. There are a host of good things we could do that could fill the schedules of multiple staff people. Trying to do it all or be all things to all people creates a rhythm of life that is not sustainable for the long term. These rhythms are not indicative of the rhythm of life that Jesus demonstrated with his disciples. In listening to God, we need to humble ourselves and submit and surrender the many good things in our life and schedule so that the God things can grow and bear a Kingdom harvest that is a thirty, sixty, and one hundred fold.

REFLECTION AND DISCOVERY
Questions for application in your context

1. *Read John 15:1-8. What are the branches that God is inviting you to prune so that greater fruit for the Kingdom can be produced?*

2. *Is your daily, weekly, and seasonal rhythm of life worthy of imitation by others?*

7
POLITY
The Role of the Board and Staff

But everything should be done in a fitting and orderly way.
−1 Corinthians 14:40

STORY

Navigating change in the midst of denominational structure can sometimes be a challenge. In my case, I celebrate that the polity of our denomination provides various levels of encouragement and accountability with primary missional decision-making being brought to the local level through the board (in our case, called a Consistory).

To build a disciple-making culture in our context, we understood (all too well from years of experience) that we needed to go slow - moving forward with revolutionary change at an evolutionary pace. We listened to the wise counsel offered by others in 3DM and didn't start the process from the pulpit through a sermon series. Rather we took the approach that the change must first begin with me and then move out with a few select leaders.

In the beginning, I floated a "trial balloon" by inviting a few folks from the church staff and from the board to join me in a 10-week exploratory Huddle. I invited them to explore with me the things I was reading, learning, and experiencing in order to see if the tools had merit and value to them and to our context.

At the end of the 10-week exploration season, the participants were invited to debrief and share not only their reflections on the Huddle experience but to also share the impact this experience had on their personal journey of discipleship.

During this debriefing time, the trial Huddle participants were crystal clear in their desire to continue. They shared that the combination of invitation and challenge coupled with the intimacy and accountability that was experienced by the group was something that many had been longing for but had not experienced previously in the church. Now, many years later, almost 100% of the primary staff (mostly part-time in our context) as well as a significant number of our revolving board participants have either journeyed with a missional community or experienced life on life discipleship in a Huddle.

RESOURCES AND TOOLS

In addition to the books and resources of 3DM, I took advantage of the insights and encouragement of a certified 3DM Coach. As mentioned earlier, I also journeyed with Dave Cheadle (a Missional Community planting partner) and a few others participating in a two-year Learning Community that provided encouraging support and relevant consultation that we desperately needed. The two-year Learning Community delivered a combination of teaching, hands-on training, and tactics that strategically guided us through these important early years.

Throughout the process, I (along with those I was Huddling) affirmed the biblically based resources and Scripture-illuminating tools of 3DM that opened our eyes to walk more intentionally the road of discipleship.

I have appreciated the invitation and most importantly the challenge to live a life worthy of imitation. In addition, I celebrate the seamless way in which 3DM's many decades of experience have been applied cross-denominationally in building a discipling culture in a variety of contexts.

As it relates to polity, in my context as a minister of Word and Sacrament as a part of the Reformed Church in America, I along with our staff and board celebrate the way in which the teaching and tools of 3DM function effectively within our theology and structure.

As an example, here is a bit of information about the Reformed Church in America and how their theology, leadership, mission, and vision are being lived out at our local congregational level:

OUR MISSION

The Reformed Church in America is a fellowship of congregations called by God and empowered by the Holy Spirit to be the very presence of Jesus Christ in the world.

Our shared task is to equip congregations for ministry—a thousand churches in a million ways doing one thing—following Christ in mission, in a lost and broken world so loved by God.

OUR VISION

Imagine...

Laity and pastors unleashed, hungry for ministry; congregations mission-minded and inviting, authentic and healing, growing and multiplying, alert to the opportunities around them.

Imagine...

Classes and synods as communities of nurture and vision—accountable, responsible, sustained by prayer, alive to the Spirit.

Imagine...

A denomination, locally oriented, globally connected, that prays in many languages and beholds the face of Christ in every face; a denomination renewed and renewing, raising up leaders, always directing its resources toward the front lines of ministry.

Imagine...

Hurts being healed, the lost being found, the hungry being fed, peace healing brokenness, hope replacing despair, lives transformed by the love of Jesus Christ.

Imagine...

The Reformed Church in America, engaging the world.

Mission and vision statements only provide a part of the picture. As we know too well, the devil is often in the details. So if you are interested in further details including references from the *Book of Church Order*, please see Appendix #2: Roles and Responsibilities and Appendix #3: Board Equipping located at the back of this book.

Crossing Contexts

In spring 2016, I was invited to participate in a 14-day equipping trip in Latvia and Estonia. While I was invited specifically to share the disciple-making resources of 3DM, I was also invited to share examples of how we organize our board as a part of an equipping weekend facilitated by Bill Hoyt with the Baltic Pastoral Institute.

It is interesting how God moves and how he continues to lead by the Holy Spirit. As a part of this trip, I was strongly encouraged to include in this book a few details of our structure, as they appeared to be particularly relevant to the *oikos*/Family on Mission-sized congregations that are predominant in the Baltic context.

In brief, the Faith Community Church Board structure is organized as follows:

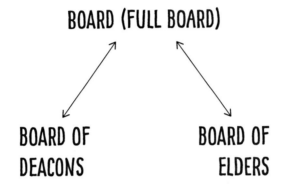

BOARD (FULL BOARD)

BOARD OF DEACONS

BOARD OF ELDERS

The larger full Board and the smaller boards of Deacons and Elders, which make up the full Board, are organized as follows:

- **Board/Agenda Focus:** A primary emphasis on Discipleship, Equipping in the Board's Role, and Prayer, seeking to address only those items that cannot be handled by an empowered (delegated Authority and Responsibility) Board, Staff or Ministry team. This = "Only the big stuff!"

- **Deacon/Agenda Focus:** Defined Mission Priorities (gathered Worship, Discipleship, Missions & Service, and Stewardship) and the Empowerment and Encouragement of Ministry Teams under their oversight so that they are enabled to do "ministry" consistent with the Vision and Mission of Faith Community Church.

- **Elder/Agenda Focus:** Defined Mission Priorities (gathered Worship, Discipleship, Missions & Service, and Stewardship) and the Empowerment and Encouragement of Ministry Teams under their oversight so that they are enabled to do "ministry" consistent with the Vision and Mission of Faith Community Church.

Undergirding the structure referenced above are the application and understanding of authority, responsibility, and the representative principle. While specific details are included in the Appendix, a bottom-line summary of the nature of authority, responsibility, and the representative principle in our structure is as follows:

- affirms Jesus Christ as the ONLY Head of the Church

- affirms and delegates authority to the priesthood of all believers

- recognizes that those in office are all on an equal standing and of an equal voice

- states that those who serve as ministers serve alongside the other office holders as simply "an elder of a special kind"

These statements of polity coupled with a vision that invites and encourages us to *imagine* as we live into a mission reflecting "a thousand churches in a million ways doing one thing—following Christ in mission, in a lost and broken world so loved by God" is both empowering and encouraging.

With this denominational structure in place and in mind, the collective discernment of the full board and staff is vitally important as we listen to God's voice and the direction of the Holy Spirit to announce the good news of Jesus' Savior-hood and extend Christ's Lordship within our unique ministry context throughout the world.

I hope this chapter serves as an example of how the biblically rooted resources and tools of 3DM have been considered, reviewed, and implemented within one particular context. While your particular context will undoubtedly vary, I hope our experience will encourage you to look for opportunities to work within your existing structure to implement a disciple-making culture relevant in your context.

REFLECTION AND DISCOVERY
Questions for application in your context

1. *Look again at 1 Corinthians 14:40 quoted at the beginning of this chapter. Now read the entire chapter. Would folks in your context tend to quote verse 40 (encouraging that "everything should be done in a fitting and orderly way"), or would they more broadly quote from the theme of chapter 14 which encourages prophesy and the building up of the church?*

   - *NOTE: SEE verse 26 - What then shall we say, brothers and sisters? When you come together, each of you has a hymn, or a word of instruction, a revelation, a tongue or an interpretation. Everything must be done so that the church may be built up.*

2. *What are some of the organization, structural, or polity realities you need to consider as you seek to implement revolutionary change at an evolutionary pace in your context?*

8
PARTNERING
Relationally Living out the Big Mission

Though one may be overpowered, two can defend themselves. A cord
of three strands is not quickly broken.
—Ecclesiastes 4:12

But you will receive power when the Holy Spirit comes on you; and you
will be my witnesses in Jerusalem, and in all Judea and Samaria,
and to the ends of the earth.
—Acts 1:8

STORY

Living along the Front Range in Colorado is one of those blessings you celebrate every day—beautiful views, an abundance of recreational options, and 300+ days of sunshine a year are constant reminders of God's many blessings. The Front Range also is a place where independent folks tend to come. Perhaps we are similar to those who travelled here in decades past who had a frontier "I'm gonna make it no matter what" drive. Perhaps this same spirit leads many of us in our own day to strive to make it on our own.

In the Senior Access Missional Community that we host every Thursday from 10am to noon, we focus first and foremost on being an extended family on mission. We recognize that as we age, our worlds tend to get smaller, and as a result relational connections and community become more and more important.

Similarly, as a small church on a Big Mission, we have realized we do not have the resources of larger churches or other organizations in our community. In terms of geography and what we discussed in the previous chapter on denominational polity, we also recognize that we are just one of a small collection of denominational churches smattered across the Front Range. As a result, because of distance we have not experienced the kind of support networks or resources that are available in other parts of the country in our denomination.

To help us to survive, we have taken on another practice that was common in the frontier and have taken on a bit of barn-raising approach to ministry. I can't help but picture the barn-raising scene in one of my favorite musicals, *Seven Brides for Seven Brothers*. While everything starts out with a common goal firmly in mind, by the end of the barn-raising scene, everything literally falls apart as feuding factions and families direct their energies at one another as opposed to the mission at hand. This kind of feuding can sometimes take place with churches in the community. Rather than be separated, we have intentionally entered into partnerships that leverage resources across churches seeking to move forward the greater vision of ushering in the Kingdom of heaven on earth in our community.

RESOURCES AND TOOLS

In the first few years in Littleton, I observed that collaborative partnerships and the sharing of resources amongst churches was generally not the norm. From my years in western Michigan, I had been blessed to experience the benefits and resource-sharing approach of an organization envisioned by Virgil Gulker (a Professor at Hope College who I was blessed to meet years later) called *Love INC* (In the Name of Christ).

Within a few weeks of landing in Littleton, I received an invitation from Nancy Parks of the St. Francis Cabrini Parish to come to a gathering to hear a vision of a partnering ministry that would connect the Church (capital

"C") together in order to meet needs and to provide resources for the broader community.

After many months of discussion, this partnering vision of Nancy Parks became *Love INC of Littleton*. While development and collaborative efforts are ongoing, this has been one tangible expression of partnering that has led our small church to participate with other churches in the Big Mission. At present we partner, resource, and and in some cases lead a number of gap ministries of *Love INC of Littleton* including *Senior Access, Haven's Hope* diaper ministry, *Severe Weather Shelter Network (which has expanded significantly and in late 2016 formed its own 501c3)*, as well as *Giving Heart* (which was launched through one of our church planting partnerships in Englewood, Colorado).

Even more broadly, as a part of the 3DM Learning Community conducted in Denver, I along with Dave Cheadle, Peter Holwerda, and Craig Broek (of the Christian Reformed Church) partnered and journeyed together in a 2-year process where we worked together for four days every six months alongside a host of denominations, non-denominational, and Para church organizations who were seeking to implement a disciple-making culture in their context.

The 3DM Learning Community and the partnering experience with *Love INC of Littleton* and with the *Severe Weather Shelter Network* have helped our congregation as a whole to look beyond ourselves to the Bigger Mission that God is unfolding in our midst. While this picture can be applied in a host of contexts, we are celebrating that while our congregation is small enough to care, alone we tend to not be big enough to dare. In partnership with other churches and organizations, the combined resources under-girded with spiritual capital from above are revealing the Kingdom of heaven on earth.

I am blessed to be a part of an emerging 3DM Hub in the Denver area.

Over the years, by God's grace and the guidance of the Holy Spirit, the leadership team has evolved to reflect a diversity of faith expressions represented across our geography. Our local 3DM workshops and Learning Communities have included and been led by folks from the Reformed Church in America, the Assembly of God, Missouri Synod Lutherans, Anglicans, and the Christian Reformed Church, to name a few. These partnering experiences have impacted us greatly. As a result, we have grown to the point that we don't even consider moving forward in ministry alone.

This partnering perspective is also demonstrated in our invitation and developing partnership with our sister denomination the Christian Reformed Church. At present, not only are we partnering with them in disciple-making and continuing learning opportunities, but we have also opened up our facility and are living out a new paradigm of two churches in the same building. This is an example of multiple wineskins residing and functioning effectively in the same wine cellar. Not unlike the scene from *Seven Brides for Seven Brothers*, sometimes this close proximity and partnership creates tension. But at the bottom line, all these tensions tend to fade as we together witness the broader expression and picture of God's Kingdom all around us.

In many ways, partnering is all about living the many "one anothers" of scripture. As a small church on a Big Mission we are Christian disciples who <u>welcome</u> one another, <u>know</u> one another, <u>care</u> for one another, <u>pray</u> for one another, <u>support</u> one another, and <u>encourage</u> one another as we are being transformed by the Holy Spirit through the rushing waters of the Word of God more fully into the character and competencies of Jesus Christ.

REFLECTION AND DISCOVERY

Questions for application in your context

1. *Consider Acts 1:8. Is it possible to be a witness to your Jerusalem, your Judea and Samaria, and to the ends of the earth without partnering?*

2. *Consider Ecclesiastes 4:12. Does your ministry tend to function alone or as a cord of multiple strands that is not quickly broken?*

3. *Who are the churches and Para church organizations that you are currently partnering and sharing resources with in your context?*

9
PIPELINE
Recruiting, Equipping, Deploying, Debriefing

After this the Lord appointed seventy-two others and sent them two by two ahead of him to every town and place where he was about to go. He told them, "The harvest is plentiful, but the workers are few. Ask the Lord of the harvest, therefore, to send out workers into his harvest field.
—Luke 10:1-2

STORY

I didn't grow up in the church. While my parents and family were practicing believers in Jesus Christ, when I was about five years old, our family dropped out of church all together. Though the term "Dones" didn't exist back in the late 1960s, for all practical purposes that's what we were.

My parents had been very active in the church, in disciple-making, and in church-planting in particular. I don't recall much from these years. Most of my memories from the church we attended in the country were of my mom and dad trying to keep me, the youngest of their five children, from squirming during the service by feeding me with quarter-sized mints that I recall tasting like Pepto-Bismol.

While I strongly considered myself to be a practicing believer who had given my life to Jesus as a young child, I didn't grow up in the church or remember ever being discipled for the most part. In fact, other than the mints (which I recall sometimes had lint on them from being in my dad's pocket for many weeks), my only other recollections are of singing *Deep and Wide*, of Bible stories demonstrated on a felt board, and of going to a Bible Camp one summer when I was about ten years old.

All this to say, I don't ever recall being discipled in any other fashion than hearing a message and going to a few a classes. In my college years at Hope, I was drawn to the chapel services, which in those days were sparsely attended. To this day, I consider Dimnent Chapel to be a "thin place" where it seemed like heaven was reaching down to us as we were reaching up to God. This is where I began to sense more keenly that God was speaking to me an inviting me to do something about it.

After my wife Elyse and I married, we joined Trinity Reformed Church in Holland, Michigan, and began a relationship that years later would lead me to seminary. Mike VanDornik was the pastor at Trinity, and he would later serve as my mentor through the long 8-year journey of seminary. For the most part, whether it was at Trinity or at the Springdale Baptist Church in Arkansas, where we lived for a number of years, discipleship pretty much took the same form for me: go to church, attend a Sunday School class and/or a small group in order to achieve the understood outcome of becoming a disciple.

The one exception to the above story was a season in which I journeyed with Jim Dannenberg, a retired postal service worker, who invited me and a few others to go through the Navigators 2:7 series. In hindsight, this brief formative season many years ago best reflected what I am now doing as I walk alongside others as a Barnabas-like encourager in the vehicles of Huddle and Missional Communities.

RESOURCES AND TOOLS

As a 3DM coach, I invite pastors to tell me about the processes they utilize to make disciples. While some pastors will flat out state that they don't have a process, others will share stories of engaging people in worship to hear their preaching while also encouraging them to go deeper in small group and Sunday School settings.

During a recent trip to the Baltics, on one particular night in Tartu, Estonia, we were invited to enjoy dinner in the home of one of our hosts. Our host shared about their church and the different ways they had done small groups in previous seasons. He shared that they had recently begun a home-group approach that focused mostly on welcoming newcomers and sharing a meal together while also including some prayer and a brief time in scripture. I couldn't help but smile and affirm how they were discovering the vehicle of Missional Communities meeting in homes. Our host also shared about how, for deeper discipleship, they were using DNA groups to intentionally develop disciples and future leaders. I smiled again as what he described sounded in many ways like the vehicle of a Huddle.

While the disciple-making approaches encountered in my youth and even utilized in my early years as a pastor could best be described as a fuzzy disciple-making process, the recent years have demonstrated a more intentional process of Recruiting, Equipping, Deploying, and Debriefing disciple-making leaders that God is elevating as persons of peace in my context.

As a part of the 3DM Learning Community, I began to assess our leadership development Pipeline. Below is a simple picture of what a disciple-making leadership development pipeline looks like.

LEADERSHIP PIPELINE

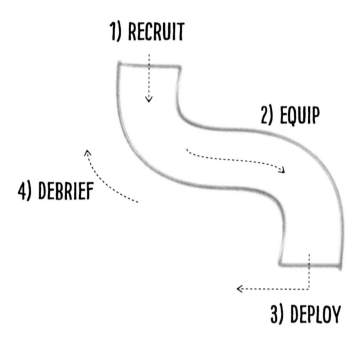

As I mentioned, our Pipeline was pretty fuzzy. But over a few years, our pipeline evolved as we began to focus and live into each section. Let me describe each section briefly:

> **1) Recruit:** Recruiting is not about filling vacant roles on ministry teams, in the nursery, or something similar. Rather, it is about doing what Jesus did when he went to the Father seeking the names of those prepared in advance to be disciples (Luke 6:12). Recruiting is seeking the people the Father is preparing and providing and then extending an invitation for them to follow.

2) Equip: Once folks accept an invitation to be discipled, we need to clarify what it was that we were going to do to make disciples who live lives that resemble the lives of the people we read about in scripture. The resources of 3DM and the vehicle of Huddle provide the framework for our disciple-making approach—especially *Building a Discipling Culture*, the *Huddle Leaders Guide*, and the *Huddle Participant Book*. Not only did these resources provide information, but in addition and more importantly, my experiences in a Huddle and then leading others through Huddles provided the example that we imitated and invited others to reproduce.

3) Deploy: Very quickly in the discipling process, Jesus deployed his disciples (as referenced in Luke 10:1-2) in order for them to put into practice the discipling life he was modeling. In our context, we also needed spaces for the disciples to practice. Through a combination of leading within the context of the Huddle itself along with opportunities to lead and teach within existing Missional Community gatherings, safe places were provided for effective training that would lead to the future deployment of growing disciple-makers. Practice with feedback is critical in the development of both character and competency.

4) Debrief: Feedback is helpful and necessary for development and refinement of our heart and our skills. Jesus' life-on-life approach of walking daily with the disciples provided countless opportunities for questions, feedback, reflection, and continuing practice. Our approach should model his.

Over time, our virtually non-existent Pipeline began to take shape:

LEADERSHIP PIPELINE

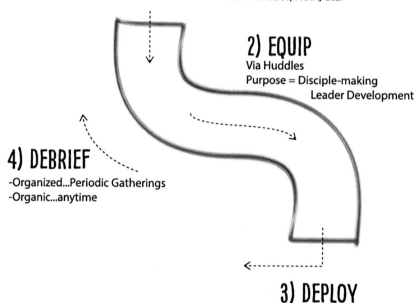

1) RECRUIT
Via gathering Vehicles of: Worship, Missional
Communities, P.O.P., etc.

2) EQUIP
Via Huddles
Purpose = Disciple-making
Leader Development

4) DEBRIEF
-Organized...Periodic Gatherings
-Organic...anytime

3) DEPLOY
-To the Place the Father calls (discernment)
-As Huddle Leaders
-As New Missional Community Leaders
-As Small Group Leaders
-As Team Leaders
-As Missional Community (church) Planters
-As unleashed Disciples to Other Areas of Ministry

As we put the disciple-making leader pipeline into practice over time, I experienced a number of areas of growth and development as a leader, and so did the culture of our church. As noted in the first section of this book, when I began stepping up as a leader who was discipling others using the vehicle of Huddle, it had an impact on me. My character and my competencies developed as I taught others.

I am continuing to grow in my sensitivity to the prompting of the Holy Spirit as I seek to hear the voice of my heavenly Father, particularly as it relates to identifying the men and women that God is placing in front of me to disciple. Mike Breen's book *Multiplying Missional Leaders* was particularly helpful in its provision of filters to pray through as I consider the names of possible people to invite to engage in a future disciple-making Huddle.

This visual includes the four "C" filters of character, chemistry, capacity, and calling. While character is undoubtedly the most important of these filters, it is important to also pray through the person's chemistry with you, the capacity to grow as well as the capacity in the person's schedule to truly live life-on-life together, as well as the person's particular sense of calling to join you in this season.

1) RECRUIT

Via gathering Vehicles of: Worship, Missional
Communities, P.O.P., etc.

1st Filter
-Character
-Competency
-Chemistry
-Calling

LEADERSHIP PIPELINE

2nd Filter
-Readiness / 2 areas
  1) Demonstrated Skill Level
  2) Experience in relation to
church
-Availability / 2 areas
  1) Current Realities
  2) Openess to Change

2) EQUIP
Via Huddles
Purpose = Disciple-making
Leader Development

Method
-Prayer
-Personal Invitation

4) DEBRIEF

-Organized...*First Friday Gatherings*
-Organic...anytime

3) DEPLOY

-To the Place the Father calls (discernment)
-As Huddle Leaders
-As New Missional Community Leaders
-As Small Group Leaders
-As Team Leaders
-As Missional Community (church) Planters
-As unleashed Disciples to Other Areas of Ministry

As I journeyed with folks in the vehicle of the Huddle, a significant *kairos* moment emerged as folks moved around the Square (another *LifeShape*) toward deployment. I began to realize that one of my areas of growth was in letting go of control of where the folks being discipled would be deployed. In short, I realized that God had far bigger plans in mind for his disciples than I did. It was not about equipping folks to be small group leaders or Sunday School teachers or the like. Rather, my role was to travel alongside as a Barnabas-like encourager as emerging disciples realized the amazing calls that God was placing on their life. In some cases this took the form of being deployed to launch and lead new missional communities, while in other cases it led to the launching of new Para church ministries. I was blessed to simply walk alongside as each person listened to the voice of God as they reflected, discussed, and put together plans for kairos moment after *kairos* moment after kairos moment.

Lastly, figuring out a new rhythm for debriefing and staying in contact with folks as the pipeline evolved was far more difficult than I had imagined. As my personal rhythm of equipping folks through Huddles developed in parallel fashion with our family rhythm of Missional Community life, it became increasingly challenging to provide encouragement and ongoing support to the many deployed disciple-making leaders in our orbit. Over time and with the counsel of other disciple-making leaders, we moved into an organized and organic approach for debriefing that fit our rhythms.

The organic (or unorganized) approach involved day-to-day interactions that tended to pop up naturally. The organic was the easy part of debriefing. The organized, however, was more challenging to develop. Eventually we started a new rhythm on the First Friday of each month gathering at our home around the fire pit (or fireplace, should Denver decide to drop one of its crazy 24-inch-plus snowstorms) as an intentional way to provide debriefing. During these gatherings we invested in relational capital and utilized a simple structure of welcoming, prayer, devotion using the daily text from God's word, and then opening up the floor for discussions of topics and situations being experienced in their disciple-making contexts.

While the pipeline is still evolving, the benefits of developing a disciple-making culture and process for intentional leader development are beginning to be seen in abundance. At a recent board and staff retreat, a number of recent additions to the board were brought up to speed on the disciple-making culture and pipeline elements that have been occurring behind the scenes around them for the last several years. It was evident that the efforts taken with a few were impacting the many. Most importantly, it was clear that the Holy Spirit is moving in our midst as we were all seeking what God was saying and what we were being invited to do about it in our context. The initial efforts to make disciples who make disciples was developing and impacting our culture in powerful ways.

REFLECTION AND DISCOVERY
Questions for application in your context

1. *If someone asked you to share your pipeline, how would you describe the process for disciple-making in your church context?*

2. *Are the recruiting efforts in your context more focused on filling spots to keep the machinery of the church running or on discipling the persons that God is placing in your orbit so that they can make future disciples? How might you need to change in these areas?*

PART 3

PURPOSEFUL DIRECTION
FOCUS, FUTURE, FUNCTION, AND FORMATIVE LANGUAGE

10
5Vs

Focusing on the Ends and Means of Ministry

"For my thoughts are not your thoughts, neither are your ways my ways,"
declares the LORD.
—Isaiah 55:8

STORY

Why are we here, where are we going, and what are we doing? These important questions often go unanswered or assumed in smaller church contexts.

In the next chapter, I will share a story that focuses a bit on the underlying or implicit values that tended to undergird and guide our small church. In this chapter, let me focus a bit on the bigger picture.

When I first came to Littleton, I took to heart the wise counsel of other pastors and did a lot of listening and visiting while changing very little publicly. As I met with people and heard their stories, their journeys, their joys and their sorrows both personally and together as a church, it became quite apparent that there was not a common understanding of why the church existed, of where we were going, or of what things that were most important for us to be doing.

My reading of Gary L. McIntosh's book *Taking your Church to the Next Level: What got you here won't get you there* had illumined me to the St. John Syndrome (referencing the seven churches in Revelation) and pointed to the reality that Faith Community Church was well beyond the entrepreneurial, organizational, and peak efficiency stages of its lifecycle. Most likely, Faith was in the institutional stage and was and rapidly approaching the decline (descent to death) stage. When I asked people what Faith Church was all about and what it was known for, the most common responses were: We are a friendly church, we are a church known for its choir and its music, or even that we are the *Pass it On* church (because we closed every service with the congregation coming together, holding hands, and singing the first verse of this 1980s campfire song).

While all of the above statements were interesting, none of them spoke with clarity of our values, our mission, or of the vision that God had given this particular community of faith.

RESOURCES AND TOOLS

Prior to becoming a pastor, I worked for nearly two decades in sales, marketing, and training. In these arenas, having a clear understanding of the desired outcomes is understood as vitally important. While the language of Mission, Vision, and Values is not new in the church, having a simple tool to articulate and keep your focus on these outcomes is helpful. So in this section I will share about a 1-page tool referred to as the 5 Vs that is used and incorporated as a strategic resource as a part of the 3DM Learning Community process.

The 5 Vs are: values, vision, vehicles, valuation, and vocabulary. Another way to look at these 5 Vs is through the lens of ends and means. The ends are the desired outcomes as expressed through values and vision. The means are the ways in which the ends will be accomplished through vehicles, valuation, and the vocabulary consistently utilized as cultured is shaped and developed.

The capacity to articulate future possibilities is a defining competence of leaders. Regardless of who lays out the imagined future—the Pastor, the Board, the Staff, or as a group—the capacity to articulate the purpose and preferred picture of the future of the ministry is an important competency to develop and demonstrate regularly.

In business, our teams spent countless hours in mission and vision sessions and on retreats as we planned the direction of the coming year and long-term future of the brand and products we provided. At the end of the day, we came to an agreement on the direction principles to guide our decision-making and investment of resources as we sought to accomplish the purpose and preferred picture of the future.

The church as a whole benefits greatly when clarity of mission, vision, and values is attained using the tool of the 5 Vs.

Before moving on, allow me to share a word about clarity and brevity: if you can't remember it, it is undoubtedly not brief or clear enough. Further, if the details of the ends of means of the ministry require a detailed workbook to understand undoubtedly further work on both clarity and brevity is in order.

Provided below is a snapshot resource you can use for understanding the 5 Vs. In the successive chapters, I'll focus on all five Vs in more detail.

THE 5Vs
Articulating the Preferred Future and how we are going to get there

2) VISION (ENDS)
Responsibility Lived Out
(Kingdom)

4) VALUATION (MEANS)

Counting what Counts:
• Qualitative - Values Focused
• Quantitative - Vision Focused
• Celebrating WINS

5) VOCABULARY
Key Words that help to
define & articulate the
culture

3) VEHICLES (MEANS)

Intentionally move us forw
the delivering of the Value:
tionship) & Vision (Respon:

1) VALUES (ENDS)
Relationship & Family Lived Out
(Covenant)

REFLECTION AND DISCOVERY
Questions for application in your context

1. *Without looking it up, what are the desired ends (values and vision) that your ministry is striving to deliver?*

2. *What are the means (the vehicles and the valuation) that your church or ministry utilizes to measure effectiveness of delivering the ends?*

3. *What are the top two are three terms (vocabulary) that are consistently utilized in articulating the direction and culture of your church or ministry?*

11
VALUES AND VISION
A Future Focus for the Ministry (the Ends)

During the night Paul had a vision of a man of Macedonia standing
and begging him, "Come over to Macedonia and help us." After Paul
had seen the vision, we got ready at once to leave for Macedonia,
concluding that God had called us to preach the gospel to them.
—Acts 16:9-10

STORY

When I was asked to interview for the pastor role at Faith Community Church, I was provided a church profile that included a list of 5 values using the acronym of F.A.I.T.H. I was encouraged to review this list and felt blessed for the hard work the leadership had done in seeking to document their values built on a foundation of the beliefs of the church.

While it is true that values are future-focused and understood as values that we aspire to live into, it took me years to realize how far the congregation as a whole needed to go to move from aspired to lived-out values.

In particular, two areas of Faith's value statements were areas where significant growth and development needed to take place: Actively making Disciples and being Harmonious in our service.

These two statements are intricately connected. The first speaks of the importance as a disciple of developing both our character (our heart as a reflection of the heart of the heavenly Father) and our competency (practicing and developing skills that Jesus taught and demonstrated with his disciples). Developing both character and competency as a disciple intersects in either beautiful or challenging ways when we bring believers together in the context of a congregation.

Systemic Change

This most easily witnessed in the context of a town meeting. At Faith, I quickly began to see how the family system tended to function. Gossip, triangulation, and backstabbing were common if not the norm. This didn't just happen in the parking lot or in the shadows of the church—it also happened in the context of town meetings. In the very first town meeting the church conducted not long after my arrival, I found it necessary to institute a short-term policy of waving the flag. I literally came to all town meetings with a flag I could raise (kind of like a caution flag in racing) to help people become visually aware of when their comments were moving beyond harmonious to being aggressive and attacking.

While this helped, you do not change a culture or a family system overnight - particularly not with the simple waving of a caution flag in the middle of public meetings. Changing a culture takes years and happens over time through life-on-life individual discussions that take place day after day.

The first place we started, was working with the leaders—staff and the board of the church. During this time the board-equipping resources mentioned previously and found in the appendix were developed and taught. While this journey from aspired to realized values has been long and difficult, I celebrate that today our family system tends to consistently demonstrate values reflected and driven from our beliefs as we demonstrate the character and the competencies of Jesus Christ.

RESOURCES AND TOOLS

Having a clear future focus on the values—the qualitative characteristics and behaviors that will consistently be demonstrated in your context— is vitally important. Similarly, having a clear future focus on the vision— the picture of the preferred future in mind—is equally if not even more important.

While Faith Community Church at least had a list of values, in reality we had no picture of their preferred future in either the form of a mission or a vision. In the absence of a defined mission or vision, it became apparent during my first year in Littleton what the implicit mission was all about. The implicit mention that they expected me to provide was leading the church to its glory days of the mid-1990s. More specifically, the goal was to lead in a way that would bring back to the church many who had left in previous years while also caring for remaining members unconditionally while allowing the dysfunctional behavior of the church family (yeah, there was a lot of that) as we sang their favorite songs.

Area #1 / Values

The values for Faith Community Church existed prior to my arrival. Over the course of many years, these values moved from being aspired to values to lived-out values.

The phrase "adaptive change" comes to mind when I think about moving to live out these values. Scott Cormode of Fuller Seminary describes adaptive change this way:

Adaptive challenges (or change) occur "when our deeply held beliefs are challenged, when the values that made us successful become less relevant, and when legitimate yet competing perspectives emerge."

Let's look at this definition. Adaptive challenges happen when we ask people to adopt new beliefs, when we hope people will pursue better values, or when we help people see that the ways that they have been doing things in the past will not work for them. Cormode further states, "... that's the job description for ministry."

The situation at Faith Community Church was not unlike so many other churches that are in the process of searching for a new pastor. They take the time to write out nicely articulated value statements as they seek to attract the pastor who will fulfill their implicit expectations. Not surprisingly, these aspired values communicated so nicely on the page are often far from the reality of what is lived out by the "family on mission."

Remember that values are an end of the ministry. Values are a vital part of the preferred future picture and provide direction for the way relationships are demonstrated and lived out on a daily basis by the covenant family.

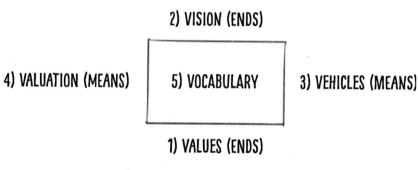

THE 5Vs
Articulating the Preferred Future and how we are going to get there

2) VISION (ENDS)

| 4) VALUATION (MEANS) | 5) VOCABULARY | 3) VEHICLES (MEANS) |

1) VALUES (ENDS)

Relationship & Family Lived Out

- *Do they describe the Covenant Community?*
- *Do they reveal the Father's heart?*
- *Do they demonstrate grace vs. law?*

As you consider your own value statements, be sure to address the questions of:

not just aspirational, but lived

- Do our value statements describe the way in which our covenant community behaves in its relationships with one another?

- Do our value statements reveal and reflect the nature of our heavenly Father's heart?

- Do our value statements express relational behavior that is based in grace, or do they tend to reflect relational behavior that is demonstrated in law?

As we addressed the questions above at Faith Community Church, the leadership sought to make these values memorable by using the acronym of F.A.I.T.H. While the primary words of the acronym (Fruitful, Active, Inspiring, Theologically Sound, and Harmonious) have remained the same since developed by the search committee in 2004, over time the value statements have been modified and have incorporated some tweaks to provide greater clarity, as you see in this graphic:

2) VISION (ENDS)

| 4) VALUATION (MEANS) | 5) VOCABULARY | 3) VEHICLES (MEANS) |

1) VALUES (ENDS)

- *Fruitful* in Mission and Service
- *Actively* Making Disciples
- *Inspiring* in gathered Worship
- *Theoligically Sound* teaching Truth from God's Word
- *Harmonious* in our Service with one another

Area #2 / Vision

Over the years, I have heard a number of discussions and differing definitions of the terms mission and vision. While some people consider the terms be to somewhat interchangeable, I perceive that they are different in form and have a different function.

Bill Hoyt, speaking to the nature of the shared leadership of a pastor and the board relates to the mission and vision, writes:

> A healthy church knows and accepts its God-given reason for being. A healthy church knows its Mission is to make disciples. It's the work of the Pastor and Board to keep the Mission before the people. While the Mission is the church's God-given purpose, their Vision is a description in words of what it looks like for that church to accomplish its Mission. The Vision is a word picture of a preferred future. A Vision is never what is now; it is always about something yet to be that would clearly indicate they are effectively making disciples.

Hoyt goes on to state "it is the work of the Pastor and Board to see that a clear, concise and compelling Mission and Vision is created and communicated to the people of the church".

Therefore, under this second v of vision, we will include both a mission and vision. Most importantly, we are seeking to articulate a clear picture of the preferred future that can be shared, understood, and remembered by others.

At Faith Community Church, we have a mission as well as a vision statement. Both are considered to be a part of the ends of ministry and provide both the purpose (mission) and picture (vision) that we are seeking to live into as the Kingdom of heaven is realized on earth in our context. While these statements are vitally important for the congregation, they are even important for the staff and the board because they enable us to say no to opportunities and ideas that come up on a daily basis while we make front-line decisions regarding the ministries of the church.

It's helpful to remember that since vision is an end of the ministry, it also provides a guide and a picture of the stewardship entrusted to the board and pastor as they share leadership and live out the responsibility that has been entrusted to them in their particular context.

2) VISION (ENDS)
Responsibility Lived Out

- *Does it reflect the Kingdom - expressing UP, IN, and OUT?*
- *Can it be given a current emphasis to refresh and articulate regularly?*

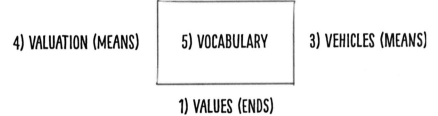

| 4) VALUATION (MEANS) | 5) VOCABULARY | 3) VEHICLES (MEANS) |

1) VALUES (ENDS)

As you consider your mission (purpose) and vision (picture) statements, be sure to address the questions of:

- Does your mission clearly communicate your purpose, and does it reflect the great commission to make disciples?

- As it relates to making disciples, does it consider the three-dimensional nature of a disciple's life as Jesus demonstrated: UP, IN, and OUT?

- Does your vision statement paint a picture that reflects the Kingdom of heaven on earth in your particular context?

- And since mission and vision statements are living statements (not static or permanent), perhaps a relevant question is whether it is time for your statements to be refreshed and given current emphasis to provide greater clarity of the picture of the preferred future?

- Finally and practically, now that you have your mission and vision statements articulated, are they being shared publicly in some form or fashion on a weekly basis?

The Board and Staff of the church developed our mission and vision statements as a group effort, and then they were affirmed as a whole by the congregation. Our first focus was on developing of the mission statement. It was developed and refined over the course of many months with much discussion and after hours and hours of prayer. Interestingly, the finalized Mission statement—*Making disciples who are growing UP, IN, and OUT–No Excuses*—was developed without any previous knowledge of 3DM or the writings of Mike Breen. It was many years later when at the 3DM Discipleship & Mission Workshop that I first heard about the building of a discipleship culture where disciples demonstrate the three dimensions of UP, IN, and OUT. As you can imagine, this seemed like a pretty strong affirmation from God of the direction the Holy Spirit had been leading our church and leadership over the previous years.

Here are the Mission and Vision statements of Faith Community Church reflected in the 5V format.

2) VISION (ENDS)

Responsibility Lived Out

Mission—*Making Disciples who are growing in UP, IN, and OUT –No Excuses*

Vision—*Cultivating Missional Communities of unleashed disciples ushering in the Kingdom of God*

4) VALUATION (MEANS) | 5) VOCABULARY | 3) VEHICLES (MEANS)

1) VALUES (ENDS)

The Vision statement was developed many years after the Mission statement. Specifically, we felt the need to define and clarify the vision given a host of questions that seemed to be percolating both within the body and with the staff. As a small church on a Big Mission, it became more and more important for us to be clear as a leadership team and as church that we were not in a position to be all things to all people. Rather, we needed to deliver the mission (purpose) without seeking to apply the resources or strategies of a larger or mega church. As a result, the vision statement emerged quite naturally over time as we lived more and more into lightweight and low maintenances structures and strategies that fit within our context.

As the values and vision (the ends of the ministry developed) were consistently articulated over time, we began to see the preferred picture that God had been painting coming into view. As Kouzes and Posner suggested in Truth #3, people did want to know our values and beliefs, what we really care about, and what keeps us as leaders awake at night. By defining and articulating our values and vision on a weekly basis, people began to understand much more easily the story of how God has been moving in the life of Faith Community Church and our position statement as a small church on a Big Mission.

REFLECTION AND DISCOVERY
Questions for application in your context

1. In your context, do the relationships of your community of faith demonstrate your stated values?

2. As it relates to your mission, on a scale of 1-5 (with 5 being high), does your community of faith understand and live out your purpose of ministry?

3. As it relation to you vision, on a scale of 1-5 (with 5 being high), is your community of faith seeing and living out the preferred picture of your ministry?

12
VEHICLES & VALUATION
A Functional Focus for the Ministry (the Means)

Those who accepted his message were baptized, and about three thousand were added to their number that day. They devoted themselves to the apostles' teaching and to fellowship, to the breaking of bread and to prayer.
—Acts 2:41-42

STORY

Ministries, like churches, tend to go through lifecycles. Faith Community Church was no exception. Upon my arrival in Littleton in 2005, the church had been on the downward side of the bell curve of its life cycle for more than a decade. A number of ministries that had long existed had either run their course or were simply struggling to survive.

While most would not let something *like* this go on long in our work environments, in the culture of our church most people would be shocked if anyone including the pastor suggested that one of these ministries should be allowed to come to an end.

I would have done well in my earlier years of ministry to understand the importance of seeking *revolutionary change at an evolutionary pace.* As we move forward as disciples, our journey is all about transformation. This happens often slowly over time involving evolutionary (or adaptive change) steps that will eventually deliver (we trust in faith) revolutionary results both personally and in the life of the church. We are not looking for revolution, because while change can happen with revolution, usually revolutions result in a lot of blood with countless losses incurred.

I thought that we were moving slowly during my first few years at Faith by implementing very few changes at the congregational level while seeking to implement important value and vision related changes with the staff and board. But after about 3 years, the wheels began coming off the church. As we began articulating the vision and mission of making disciples and living into our aspired values, chaos began to break out, which at sometimes seemed a bit like a revolution. While there was not physical blood spilled, there were was a great deal of loss experienced with many lives negatively impacted in this season of the church.

RESOURCES AND TOOLS

These were very difficult years for the church and for me and for my family. These were also formative years in my journey of personal discipleship and as a leader. They were years that you look back on and with hindsight understanding how much God has been teaching both you and the church shaping my personal and our collective character and competency as disciples of Jesus Christ.

During these years, I didn't have an understanding of vehicles or valuation as articulated in this book. A vehicle gets you from point A to B, while valuation focuses on the counting of what counts.

In the typical church, a number of vehicles are intended to be a Means of moving the congregation and the community from point A to point B— from where you are at present to the purpose and preferred picture that God has shown you through the values and vision.

As a small church in the institutional stage of its lifecycle, vehicles that have in some cases existed for many years are attempting to move people from point A to B without the resources needed. In short, they look like a Model T Ford moving on a California Interstate—not only out of place, but also ineffective and potentially dangerous.

In other cases (perhaps often), we have a vehicle that works but fails to resource itself effectively. Using the same image as above, a vehicle on the California Interstate that doesn't have enough gas, horsepower, or even has a flat tire is ineffective in caring carry people to the intended destination (in our church's case, the vision and values).

Especially with churches in the institutional or decline stages of their lifecycle, we are unconsciously continuing to use vehicles that worked well in previous generations of the church, but are no longer very effective.

Therefore, knowing and effectively resourcing your primary vehicles to move your ministry toward your values and vision is vitally important.

Area #3 / Vehicles
In articulating your vehicles, be sure to answer with clarity the following questions:

What Vehicles are we currently using to deliver the vision and the values?
While this might seem obvious, in churches that have been around a few generations, this isn't so simple to answer. Be sure to name them all. Also, realize that when you are in the institutional phase of the lifecycle, everything that has ever existed is often perceived to be important and implicitly expected to resourced and managed. Often these implicit expectations are not addressed, resulting in frustration and corresponding assumptions that the pastor will pick up and carry these expectations as part of their role. In smaller churches, the burden of carrying these implicit and unrealistic expectations by the pastor is unsustainable. Over time, the

cart of ministry becomes far too heavy for the horse (the pastor) or even a team of horses to pull. The result is exhaustion, burnout, and even the death of the horse as the pastor choose to exit ministry altogether.

Can we effectively drive these vehicles?
Said another way, is this vehicle lightweight and low maintenance so that anyone could drive it? If the vehicle requires an advanced degree in theology to lead or run, we are likely making the job description for this role unsustainable.

Are there vehicles that we are using that need to be brought into the shop for an overhaul or need to be rebuilt or redesigned entirely?
This is often overlooked and can be the case in churches that have been around a while. This is an important part of the shared leadership of the board with the pastor and staff as they identify and resource these kinds of ministry vehicle overhauls.

The last question speaks to the nature of your pipeline of discipleship:
Do you have enough leaders to drive the existing vehicles as well as the new vehicles that need to be developed in order to accomplish the vision and values?

3) VEHICLES (MEANS)

Intentionally move us forward in the delivering of the Values *(Relationship)* & Vision *(Responsibility)*

- *What vehicles are we currently using to deliver the Vision & Values?*
- *Can we effectively drive these Vehicles?*
- *Which vehicles do you need to rebuild or redesign?*
- *Do you have enough leaders to drive current or new vehicles?*

2) VISION (ENDS)

4) VALUATION (MEANS)

5) VOCABULARY

1) VALUES (ENDS)

Given the lifecycle of our church, over the years we have whittled down the number of vehicles to a more manageable few that can be more effectively resourced in a lightweight and low-maintenance way. They include:

Public Space - size

- Gathered Worship: This vehicle is our every Sunday gathering of the family on mission. It functions as a place of gathering and praise that reminds us of our place in the connecting story of God's Word as we celebrate stories of our journey toward the values and vision that God has given us together.

- Missional Communities (Social Space-sized groups): These larger-than-small-group-sized gatherings intentionally practice rhythms of UP, IN, and OUT. We have found that these vehicles become more effective places for connecting visitors and newcomers who want to explore what the family on mission is all about. Because of their larger size and *oikos* (home) based approach, new folks are more naturally invited (OUT) and welcomed through their approach of food and fellowship (IN). They begin to understand the undergirding foundation of the group as they naturally experience prayer and brief study (UP), which usually happens around the table.

- Small Groups (larger Personal Space-sized groups): These meet at various times throughout the week and often function as UP and IN development vehicles of the ministry. We celebrate that over time through evolution (not revolution), many *NOT ALL* small groups have evolved to include UP, IN, and OUT discipleship dimensions.

- Huddles (smaller Personal Space-sized groups): Most significantly, Huddles have been added to serve as the primary disciple-making and equipping vehicle. As stated previously, disciple-making was something we assumed was happening. But when we started to assess our current state, we realized that our assumptions were inaccurate both in terms of fulfilling our mission and vision as well as our values. As a result, we invested significant effort to refine my schedule as the senior leader in order to invest time more intentionally to develop and implement this vital means of ministry.

3) VEHICLES (MEANS)

2) VISION (ENDS)

4) VALUATION (MEANS)

5) VOCABULARY

1) VALUES (ENDS)

Gathered Worship (Public Space)
- *Faith Church / Sunday 9:15am*
- *CenterPoint Church / Saturday 6pm*
- *APEX Church / Sunday 11am*

Missional Communities (Social Space)
- *Senior Access / Thursday 10am*
- *3DMondays / 1st and 3rd Monday 6:30pm*
- *R3 Women's MC / Wednesday 7pm*
- *Youth / Thursday 6:30pm*

Small Groups (Personal Space - larger)
- *Small but Mighty / Wednesday 7pm*
- *Men of Faith / Saturday 7:30am*
- *Monday Noon / Monday 12pm*
- *Tuesday Evening / Tuesday 6pm*

Huddles (Personal Space - smaller)
- *3DMondays / 2nd & 4th Monday 6:30pm*
- *Front Range Leaders / Wednesday 10am every week*

Area #4 / Valuation

Valuation is another means of moving us forward by specifically helping us to know when we are bearing fruit that fulfills the values and the vision. In valuation we are intentionally identifying a few areas to measure that truly matter. Stated more plainly, in valuation we are counting what counts.

From a denominational perspective, there are relatively few items that we are tasked to count—primarily worship attendance, baptisms, and financial information. Our local denominational group of churches challenged us to add a few additional measurements to our list. After a host of discussions of our church board using Bill Hoyt's book *Counting what Counts* as a guide, we identified a larger list of items we sensed were important for us to measure in helping us to assess our effectiveness in delivering the ends of the ministry in terms of our values and vision.

It is interesting to note that, in some circles, the discussion of counting in the church can be met with resistance. This was definitely the case in our context (both at the board and local denominational level). The text from Acts 2 shared at the beginning of this chapter is just one reminder of the many examples where the counting of numbers is reflected as a part of the biblical witness.

As you consider your valuation measures, consider the following questions:

- What are you currently counting both qualitatively (to show that your values are being demonstrated as behavior) and quantitatively (to show that your vision is being realized)?

- What other measurements do you need to add to the list to demonstrate that you are delivering the things of the Kingdom that Jesus would count as important? (i.e.: UP, IN, OUT, baptisms, missional community connections, etc.)

- How often does your community celebrate these wins of the ministry?

4) VALUATION (MEANS)

2) VISION (ENDS)

Counting what Counts

- *Qualitative—Values Focused*
- *Quantitative—Vision Focused*
- *Celebrating WINS*

5) VOCABULARY

3) VEHICLES (MEANS)

1) VALUES (ENDS)

Questions:
- *What are you currently counting?*
- *Do your metrics measure the things Jesus counts?*
- *Does your community know how to win?*

As I stated earlier, coming up with our Faith Community Church valuation measures involved some lengthy discussion by the board. During these discussion, while many on the board understood the importance of counting what counts, some folks required deeper reflection and time of discussion in order to affirm the below provided list. The measurements can also be modified over time as your grow in your clarity of the direction that God is providing. That said, here are the items we currently count:

- Qualitatively: Qualitative measurement that demonstrates the delivery of values can be challenging. We have chosen to look at two areas to determine if we are demonstrating our desired values:

    o First, we invite our community to annually complete a Three-Dimensional Disciple Self-Assessment. As stated previously in this book, we use the character and competency questions found in Building a Discipling Culture to help us measure how the behavior of the disciples in our midst are growing, developing, and moving forward toward our documented values. See Appendix II or go to www.smallchurchbigmission.org.

    o Second, taking the pulse of the community and listening to the stories being lived out and shared is another qualitative indicator. As we listen to the conversations being shared, we ask ourselves if they are reflective of our values. Over time, we have moved into publicly sharing these stories on a weekly basis through Kingdom Moments as a form of testimony for the entire community to hear.

- Quantitatively: Quantitative measurements tend to focus in areas to determine if we are moving forward toward our mission (purpose) and vision (preferred picture). Note that we specifically are looking at measurements for the vehicles previously identified:

    o # of Baptisms (both adult and infant, in our case) and the # of new disciples desiring to be recognized as a part of our family on mission (membership or, in our case, what we refer to as covenant disciples of Jesus who are journeying with us at Faith)

why did they fund?
were necessary
these

- # of Missional Communities and how many folks are participating in these Social Space-sized gatherings

- # of Small Groups and how many folks are participating in these Personal Space-sized gatherings

- # of leaders being engaged in disciple-making Huddles. This is our primary pipeline for leader development.

- # of emerging missional community and church planters being deployed

- In terms of stewardship, we also look at the percentage of giving that is being provided by folks in the family. This is determined by looking at the average giving of a family as a percentage of the household income demographics for the community around the church property.

- # of people in worship attendance.

- <u>Celebrating Wins:</u> Over time we realized that we needed to do a much better job of celebrating the progress made and forward movement experienced in the midst of our community in terms of our vision and values. Given who we are as people and in particular, and given where we were in the church lifecycle, we needed to learn and practice the celebration of wins. We have added two primary areas to help us recognize and share the many praises to God taking place in our midst.

  - Family Reunions: Once every quarter we have an intentional celebration of story telling and celebration where we focus on all three areas of UP, IN, and OUT. This is a time that begins in worship as hear multiple stories of praise and of growth and where we celebrate the sacraments of baptism and communion. After the service the worship and praise continues as we gather for a church-wide dinner around tables where more and more God stories are shared on an informal basis.

  - Kingdom Moments: As the disciple-making culture evolved, more and more stories were crying out to be heard. This moved us to begin including a weekly five-minute Kingdom moment as a part of our gathered worship each Sunday. We utilize the Kingdom moment as a time of testimony in which we focus on our Mission of making disciples who are growing UP, IN, and OUT – no excuses. On a given week, we focus on one area of the mission, either an UP, IN, or OUT, by inviting someone from the community to share a relevant story. These have been particularly effective in both helping us celebrate what God is doing and also in evolving the culture more toward a culture of disciple-making.

4) VALUATION (MEANS)

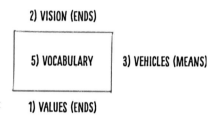

Counting what Counts

A. **Qualitative—Values Focused**
   -3D Disciple Assessment, Up, In, Out
   -Community Behavior / lived out

B. **Quantitative—Vision Focused**
   • # Baptisms & New Disciples
   • # Missional Communities
   • # engaging in Missional Communities
   • # engaging in Small Groups
   • # of Discipling Leaders in Huddles
   • # of emerging MC Plants / MC's
   • % of Giving (Financial Capital)
   • # engaged in Worship

C. **Celebrating WINS**
   • Faith Family Reunions
   • Kingdom Moments (testimonies) weekly

With the Vehicles and Valuation – the Means for developing the ministry defined, we can more easily see and celebrate the fruit that God is making grow in various ways throughout community as we together usher in the the Kingdom of heaven on earth.

In a small church on a Big Mission, just as in a small business, people want to know that you have integrity and are serious and have every intention of delivering on the promises articulated in the vision and values. To deliver these promises, it is our responsibility to insure that the vehicles are running without flat tires and delivering results that are measurable as we help to expand the Kingdom of heaven on earth.

REFLECTION AND DISCOVERY

Questions for application in your context

1. *What valuation measurements are used in your context?*

2. *Do these measurement areas provide an indication of your effectiveness of delivering your vision and values?*

3. *Make a list of the vehicles that you intentionally utilize to move people and the community forward in delivering vision and values.*

4. *Is every vehicle noted in the above list effectively resourced? Which vehicles need some work or maybe even an overhaul?*

13
VOCABULARY
Formative Language for Shaping the Culture

The quiet words of the wise are more to be heeded
than the shouts of a ruler of fools.
—Ecclesiastes 9:17

Words from the mouth of the wise are gracious,
but fools are consumed
by their own lips.
—Ecclesiastes 10:12

STORY

In my business and vocational ministry contexts, one thing has consistently remained true. The more brief the time of communication with the listener, the more necessary it is to be prepared, clear, and concise in my language to insure the message is understood.

As I write this paragraph, I am working on a message that will be delivered as the baccalaureate message to the upcoming graduating class and their families of my college alma mater. Given the venue and the time limits placed on this message, it requires more preparation time to refine the vocabulary used to insure clarity.

In preparation for this message, while the time limit was a factor, even more important was my consideration of my values and vision as well

117

as the values and vision of the college. Personally, as a disciple of Jesus Christ, I highly value the hearing and responding to God's voice. Given the scholastic nature of the audience, I also sensed the importance of communicating life-long learning. In terms of vision, I want to communicate a message that demonstrates carrying the Kingdom to the ends of the earth because this picture is shared both in Scripture as well as the college mission statement.

As the initial drafts of the message unfold on the screen, they also include examples of vehicles as well as valuation. Over time and after multiple drafts, specific vocabulary began to rise to the service to insure that the message would be understood

What's my point? Especially when time is limited, concise, clear, and consistent vocabulary is needed. Furthermore, the use of concise, clear, and consistent vocabulary should not be limited to only those situations when time is limited.

I was invited to facilitate the leadership of *Giving Heart*, an OUT reach ministry that was launched from the CenterPoint missional community church plant which was working in partnership with the local *Love INC* affiliate. The leadership team spent a significant amount of time clarifying and stating that their ministry purpose was to serve those who are "entangled in poverty." This phrase is significant as it both helps to inform volunteers of a root cause of the clients they serve in the ministry while also communicating to the community and to the client that they are valued. All of this was stated without using the term of "homelessness."

must be more than finding housing ...

In this same ministry, "transformation" is another important term they determined needed to be consistently utilized. For the *Giving Heart* ministry, transformation is a process of growing into the character and competencies of Jesus Christ. The definition and clarification of this term was important as it came directly out of discussions of both mission and vision. Their mission and vision was not simply to provide resources and fill gaps for those entangled in poverty; rather, their purpose and preferred picture involved a process of transformation for those who were entangled in poverty demonstrating the character and competencies of Jesus Christ.

RESOURCES AND TOOLS

Just as it takes multiple drafts to refine the vocabulary that will be shared in the message on a Sunday morning, even greater effort and attention should be applied to the vocabulary that you use related to the ends and means of the ministry. More than any of the other Vs, vocabulary is a primary tool used in shaping. For this reason, vocabulary is listed as the fifth of the 5 Vs. It is best and often most effective to work through the first four Vs as they will provide refinement of the all-important vocabulary.

Area #5 / Vocabulary
As stated in other areas, vocabulary can be a work in process. By doing the hard word of the first four Vs, you will undoubtedly find a list of primary vocabulary emerging. This early work will elevate the specific words and phrases that should consistently be used to help shape the church culture for the future.

As you consider your culture shaping vocabulary, be sure to address the following questions:

- Do these key words and phrases help to paint a picture shaping the way we perceive the Kingdom and God's work in our world?

- Are these words and phrases acting like a mirror that helps shape community to see and be a reflection of the Kingdom of heaven on earth?

- Another way to look at the vocabulary is to consider if these words serve as a telephoto lens that help people see and be the preferred picture up close.

2) VISION (ENDS)

4) VALUATION (MEANS)

5) VOCABULARY

Key Words that help to define & articulate the culture

- *A picture—shapes the way we perceive the Kingdom and God's work*
- *A mirror—the reflects the Kingdom and God's work*
- *A lens—helps us more clearly see and be the culture and Kingdom*

3) VEHICLES (MEANS)

1) VALUES (ENDS)

Below is the Faith Community Church vocabulary. As noted before, the vocabulary pretty much flowed out of the work done in the previous areas. In particular, we recognized that some of the words we used could be misunderstood. For example, we felt it was important to speak on a regular basis to clarify that growing IN as a disciple focused on our relationships IN the community with others. Some people, tended to interpret IN as speaking of the inward aspects of their personal spiritual journey (which would actually be better understood as the UP dimension of discipleship).

good

For Faith, the following words related to our values, vision, and vehicles are frequently communicated (often weekly) and regularly utilized within our family on mission:

good

- **UP / REFLECTION:** The extent that my character *reflects* the character and the extent that my time and energy *reflect* the competencies that Jesus demonstrated with his disciples.

- **IN / RELATIONSHIPS:** The extent that I develop and engage in *relationships* that develop the character and the extent my *relationships* demonstrate the competency that Jesus

120

demonstrated with his disciples.

- **OUT / RESPONSIBILITY:** The extent my character and competency moves me to engage in the *responsibility* that Jesus gave his disciples to make disciples in their Jerusalem, Judea, and Samaria and to the ends of the earth.

- **Missional Community:** Social Space-size *oikos* extended family gatherings that demonstrate UP, IN, and OUT rhythms consistently.

2) VISION (ENDS)

5) VOCABULARY

UP / REFLECTION—extent that my character *Reflects* the Character and the extent that my time and energy *Reflect* the Competencies the Jesus demonstrated with his disciples.

IN / RELATIONSHIPS—extent I develop & engage in *Relationships* that develop the Character and the extent my *Relationships* demonstrate the Competency the Jesus demonstrated with his disciples

OUT / RESPONSIBILITY—extent my Character & Competency moves me to engage in the *Responsibilty* that Jesus gave his disciples to make disciples in their Jerusalem, Judea & Samaria and to the ends of the earth

Missional Community—Social Space size Oikos extended family gatherings that demonstrate UP, IN, and OUT rhythms consistently

4) VALUATION (MEANS)

3) VEHICLES (MEANS)

1) VALUES (ENDS)

At the beginning of this section we set out to articulate and provide focus on the ends and means of ministry using a 1-page tool. With each of the 5 V sections developed in the preceding chapters, our finalized 1-page document looks like this:

2) VISION (ENDS)

Mission—Making Disciples who are growing in UP, IN, and OUT—No Excuses

Vision—Cultivating Missional Communities of unleashed disciples ushering tin the Kingdom of God

3) VEHICLES (MEANS)

Gathered Worship (Public Space)
- Faith Church / Sunday 9:15am
- CenterPoint Church / Saturday 6pm
- APEX Church / Sunday 11am

Missional Communities (Social Space)
- Senior Access / Thursday 10am
- 3DMondays / 1st and 3rd Monday 6:30pm
- R3 Women's MC / Wednesday 7pm
- Youth / Thursday 6:30pm

Small Groups (Personal Space - larger)
- Small but Mighty / Wednesday 7pm
- Men of Faith / Saturday 7:30am
- Monday Noon / Monday 12pm
- Tuesday Evening / Tuesday 6pm

Huddles (Personal Space - smaller)
- 3DMondays / 2nd & 4th Monday 6:30pm
- Front Range Leaders / Wednesday 10am every week

1) VALUES (ENDS)

- *Fruitful in Mission and Service*
- *Actively Making Disciples*
- *Inspiring in gathered Worship*
- *Theoligically Sound teaching Truth from God's Word*
- *Harmonious in our Service with one another*

5) VOCABULARY

UP / REFLECTION—extent that my character *Reflects* the Character and the extent that my time and energy *Reflect* the Competencies the Jesus demonstrated with his disciples.

IN / RELATIONSHIPS—extent I develop & engage in *Relationships* that develop the Character and the extent my *Relationships* demonstrate the Competency the Jesus demonstrated with his disciples

OUT / RESPONSIBILITY—extent my Character & Competency moves me to engage in the *Responsibility* that Jesus gave his disciples to make disciples in their Jerusalem, Judea & Samaria and to the ends of the earth

Missional Community—Social Space size Oikos extended family gatherings that demonstrate UP, IN, and OUT rhythms consistently

4) VALUATION (MEANS)

Counting what Counts

A. **Qualitative—Values Focused**
- 3D Disciple Assessment, Up, In, Out
- Community Behavior / lived out

B. **Quantitative—Vision Focused**
- # Baptisms & New Disciples
- # Missional Communities
- # engaging in Missional Communities
- # engaging in Small Groups
- # of Discipling Leaders in Huddles
- # of emerging MC Plants / MC's
- % of Giving (Financial Capital)
- # engaged in Worship

C. **Celebrating WINS**
- Faith Family Reunions
- Kingdom Moments (testimonies) weekly

As I draw this final chapter to a close, let me emphasize that your life and your words make a difference. Your living example and the words you consistently utilize inspire and influence others and ultimately shape culture. You do make a difference, and the first step of living into the values and the vision is a step that you make yourself.

In the busy context in *which* we now live, it is vitally important that we put forth extra effort in order to define and clarify our vocabulary so we can be understood with as few words as possible.

REFLECTION AND DISCOVERY
Questions for application in your context

1. *Vocabulary is a critical tool in the development of a culture of discipleship. Do you agree or disagree? Why?*

2. *What are the key vocabulary terms that act like a telephoto lens helping others to understand your vision and values and see the Kingdom of God up close with greater clarity?*

A FINAL THOUGHT
Walking Alongside Others as a
Barnabas-like Encourager

In the introduction I shared that this book is somewhat a journal of discovery—or perhaps better stated, a chronicle of my journey of discovery of who I am, of the character that God has helped develop in me over many years, the competencies that God has developed through a variety of ministry experiences, and most specifically a reflection of the call to discipleship and mission that God has placed on my life. In the midst of this journey of discovery, I am celebrating the blessings of being small while engaging in the Big Mission of revealing the Kingdom of God.

This journey is an amazing adventure where, like the apostle Paul in Acts 16, I am beginning to sense the times when it is most appropriate to follow the traditions of the past even when they are not required (such as in the circumcision of Timothy), and the other times when the plans that we have need to be completely put aside as we follow the vision that Jesus is bringing to us (even when it means going in a totally unanticipated direction to a people group that God is determining).

I celebrate that in this journey and most especially over the last decade I have been blessed to journey with a diverse group of Christ-followers from vastly different traditions as I have witnessed God speaking through the Holy Spirit into my life. I am growing and learning more and more every day how much my Father loves me and that he desires the very best for me. Specifically, I am growing and learning and being more obedient in following the persons of peace that present themselves. In doing so, I have been invited to go to what in some cases seems to be the very ends of the earth, where I have experienced the God and been blessed beyond my wildest expectations. This journey has been an adventure—an amazing and blessed adventure of a lifetime.

In January 2016, I was invited to be with a group gathered from around the country for a four-day summit. This was a place I had never been with a several people I was meeting for the first time.

As a part of the gathering, I was provided an envelope that contained a single index card. On the card was written the name of one person who was present at the summit. We were invited to pray for the person whose name was on the card we received and encouraged to jot down words of encouragement, scripture passages, or pictures that came to mind related to this person. At the end of the time together, the cards were turned in, and then they were provided to the person whose name was written on the card.

The card that was returned to me at the end of the week shared the following:

> "It's been a joy to hear some of your story. I'm proud of you! I got a picture of you coming to a trailhead climbing a mountain. You went left while others went right. Your trail was narrow, and few walked on

it. It was harder and longer but the views were far superior. You saw no one climbing or returning. But when you got back to where the trail split, people were looking at you. They had lots of questions on what it was like and what you saw. Most wouldn't go after hearing about it, but some would go if you lead them."

Every time I read the words from the card written above, I am brought to tears as I consider the presence, love, and grace of God demonstrated to me throughout the difficult and formative years of the journey. I also remember that there are many steps of faith that lie around every corner in the journey ahead. Most importantly, this vision shared on a simple index card clarifies and helps me to picture the road ahead as I walk alongside others who would take the challenging trail if only they had a Barnabas-like encourager to walk at their side.

God, may I continue to take faith-FULL steps as I walk alongside others that bring glory and honor to your name. Amen.

An invitation to join me in the Journey
If you are a pastor or a leader in a smaller church context, I invite you to join me in this journey of a lifetime - A journey together as we put discipleship and mission back in the hands of everyday people. While the journey can be challenging, the kingdom views we will encounter demonstrate the confidence of Psalm 27:13, *I remain confident of this: I will see the goodness of the LORD in the land of the living.*

To explore small church on a BIG Mission equipping opportunities, coaching, and 3DM Learning Communities – go to www.smallchurchbigmission.org or www.3dmovements.com.

APPENDIX 1
Living as a Three-Dimensional Disciple of Jesus Christ

A Discipleship Self-Assessment Tool

At Faith Community Church our mission is to *make disciples of Jesus Christ who are growing **Up**ward and **In**ward by Reaching **Out** – No Excuses!*

This mission to make three-dimensional disciples is vitally important for realizing of our vision of *Cultivating Missional Communities of unleashed disciples who are ushering in the Kingdom of God in this place and to the ends of the earth.*

This Discipleship Self-Assessment Tool has been developed to help you identify where you are in your journey as a disciple of Jesus Christ by providing questions related to your *Character (Being like Jesus)* and your *Competency (Doing the things that Jesus did)* in the three dimensions of UP, IN, & OUT.

The Character & Competency of a Three-Dimensional Disciple:

1. *UP / REFLECTION* – To what extent does my character *Reflect* the Character of Jesus Christ? As it relates to Competency, to what extent does my time and energy *Reflect* the Competencies that Jesus taught and demonstrated in his walk with his disciples?

2. *IN / RELATIONSHIPS* – To what extent do I develop & engage in *Relationships* that develop the Character that Jesus developed with his disciples? And to what extent do my *Relationships* demonstrate the Competency that Jesus demonstrated with his disciples?

3. *OUT / RESPONSIBILITY* – To what extent does my Character move me to engage in the *Responsibility* that Jesus gave his disciples to be witnesses in their Jerusalem, Judea & Samaria and to the ends of the earth? To what extent do I effectively demonstrate this Competency as I engage in this *Responsibility*?

The purpose of this tool is to provide you with a snapshot of where you are at this moment in time. As we journey together in our life-long process of transformation, we pray that this tool help you to see how God is speaking to you and invite you to do something about it in your continuing journey as a disciple of Jesus Christ.

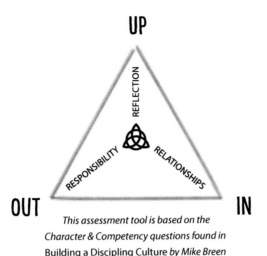

This assessment tool is based on the Character & Competency questions found in Building a Discipling Culture by Mike Breen

Three-Dimensional Disciple and the *Triquetra*

- "As we take up the challenge to become disciples of Jesus we need to model our lives after the Master. Jesus lived out his life in three relationships or dimensions: Up–with his Father; In–with his chosen followers; and Out– with the hurting world around him." *Mike Breen (3dmovements.com)*

- The Latin word *Triquetra (tri- "three" and quetrus "cornered")* originally meant "triangle" and was used to refer to various three-cornered shapes. This term can also refer to an interconnected three-loop shape (like the one provided in the center of the triangle to the left) and is often used as a symbol to reflect things or persons that are three-fold in nature.

- This symbol frequently includes a circle that goes through the three interconnected loops of the *Triquetra*. The circle reflects the unity of the whole. The circle also symbolizes God's love which envelops the whole (or the three dimensions / relationships) of the disciple.

This Discipleship Assessment Tool includes 30 statements to help you self-assess where you are in your journey as a disciple of Jesus Christ. To complete this Self-Assessment, read each statement below and then write (in the space to the left) how well you sense this statement fits you at the present time. Choose your response from the following options:

1=Never True   4=Sometimes True   6=Almost always True
2=Rarely True   5=Often True   7=Always True
3=True once in a while

1. _____ I make enough space for prayer in my daily life.

2. ____ I am intentional about making time to grow my relationships with friends and neighbors.

3. ____ I have God's heart for people who don't know Jesus.

4. ____ I am noticing God's strength and power more and more in my life.

5. ____ The physical care of my body is an important part of demonstrating my love for God.

6. ____ I make it a priority to look for opportunities to share the Gospel and my faith story with others.

7. ____ The peace of Christ rules in my heart.

8. ____ I make myself vulnerable to and trust a few other believers to hold me accountable to growth.

9. ____ I regularly make time in my schedule for relationships with

unbelievers.

10. ___ I am obedient to God's promptings.

11. ___ I am actively discipling others to help unleash them as they usher in God's kingdom.

12. ___ I have God's heart for people experiencing poverty and willingly share my time and resources.

13. ___ I find joy in praying for situations and people God lays on my heart.

14. ___ 1My family is happy and growing together as disciples of Jesus Christ.

15. ___ I claim God's vision for me as his disciple and willingly take risks to move in that direction.

16. ___ I sense my family's lifestyle is pointing more toward God.

17. ___ I am able to express and provide appropriate care and concern for my church family.

18. ___ I am able to meet and welcome new people with love and grace.

19. ___ I find it easy to receive guidance for the next steps in my faith development.

20. ___ I am effective and compassionate in resolving conflicts in the relationships God has given to me.

21. ____ God has given me a passion and vision for a specific people group.

22. ____ I celebrate that my family is on mission together, fulfilling God's vision for us as disciples of Jesus.

23. ____ I confidently practice the discipline of confrontation to maintain God's peace in my relationships.

24. ____ I can identify at least one unbeliever who is seeking a deeper relationship with me.

25. ____ I can share God's word effectively with others and help them understand its personal application.

26. ____ I celebrate God's gifts of discernment and flexibility as I work with people different from me.

27. ____ I regularly look for opportunities to connect with neighbors or co-workers who don't know Jesus.

28.____ I am comfortable acting on the leading of the Holy Spirit.

29.____ I have set appropriate boundaries in order to maintain healthy relationships.

30.____ I am an active disciple of Jesus Christ who is making other disciples of Jesus Christ.

Faith Community Church / 6228 S. Carr Court / Littleton, CO 80123 / 303.979.2468 / www.faithctr.org

SCORING AID / DISCIPLESHIP ASSESSMENT TOOL

Transfer your score responses from the Self-Assessment to the area provided below. After you have transferred your responses - add together the responses in both the "Character" and "Competency" columns for each dimension as well as your total score for each discipleship dimension (Up, In, and Out). On the reverse side of this sheet – an aid to assist you in determining your next steps is provided.

UP / Character & Competency	IN / Character & Competency	OUT / Character & Competency
___ 1 ___ 16	___ 2 ___ 17	___ 3 ___ 18
___ 4 ___ 19	___ 5 ___ 20	___ 6 ___ 21
___ 7 ___ 22	___ 8 ___ 23	___ 9 ___ 24
___ 10 ___ 25	___ 11 ___ 26	___ 12 ___ 27
___ 13 ___ 28	___ 14 ___ 29	___ 15 ___ 30

TOTALS TOTALS TOTALS

___ Up TOTAL   ___ In TOTAL   ___ Out TOTAL

Plot your scores on the Triangle on the next page - then connect the dots to view your Three-Dimensional shape as a disciple.

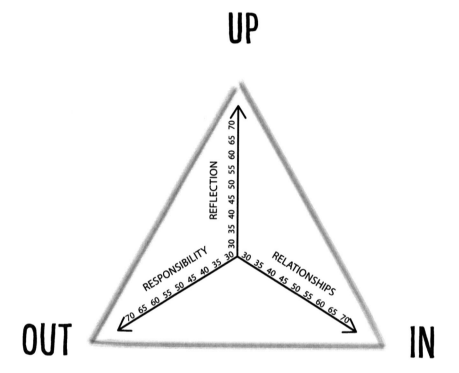

NEXT STEPS / DISCIPLESHIP ASSESSMENT TOOL

Now that you have completed your Three-Dimensional Self-Assessment, it is important to identify the next steps for your continuing journey as a disciple of Jesus Christ. This page is provided to assist you in developing your personal Discipleship Plan for the journey ahead.

In your journey to become a more balanced disciple of Jesus Christ, utilize the space below to write your personal PLAN for addressing and developing the LOWEST dimension reflected on your Three-Dimensional Disciple Assessment. Focus is important, so you are encouraged to write your personal plan in only one of the sections (the section with the lowest score from the previous page) provided below.

The Character & Competency of a Three-Dimensional Disciple:

1. *UP* / NEXT STEPS – From the previous page, look at the responses you provided to each of the UP dimension statements, paying particular attention to your lowest responses. As you look to next steps, answer: *What am I going to do about it?* Discuss with your Discipling Coach/ Small Group Leader what to include in your Discipleship Plan moving forward. My personal Discipleship Plan is:

_____

_____

_____

_____

2. *IN* / NEXT STEPS – From the previous page, look at the responses you provided to each of the IN dimension statements, paying particular attention to your lowest responses. As you look to next steps, answer: *What am I going to do about it?* Discuss with your Discipling Coach/ Small Group Leader what to include in your Discipleship Plan moving

forward. My personal Discipleship Plan is:

_____

_____

_____

_____

3. **OUT** / NEXT STEPS – From the previous page, look at the responses you provided to each of the OUT dimension statements, paying particular attention to your lowest responses. As you look to next steps, answer: *What am I going to do about it?* Discuss with your Discipling Coach/ Small Group Leader what to include in your Discipleship Plan moving forward. My personal Discipleship Plan is:

_____

_____

_____

_____

Making Disciples of Jesus Christ who are growing Upward and Inward by Reaching Out – No Excuses!
Faith Community Church / 6228 S. Carr Court / Littleton, CO 80123 / 303.979.2468 / www.faithctr.org

APPENDIX 2
A Forward View of the Board

In view of the learning of the Board in recent years, this document provides a vision and direction for the roles of the full Board, the Elders, Deacons as well as the Directional Board (or Executive Team) and how we will intentionally invest our time together

Focus of the Board

1. *Facilitated by:* President (Senior Pastor) or Vice President (in President's absence)

2. *Role Summary:* Discerning, Discussing, and Inviting the **"Will of God"** to become a reality at Faith Community Church. Our role is to provide "Oversight & Encouragement" of the staff and ministry teams as they "lead" from a position of empowered authority.

3. *Book of Church Order Summary:* The consistory shall act in all matters calling for judgment and decision which are not specifically assigned to the board of elders or to the board of deacons. The consistory shall regularly consider the nature and extent of the ministry of the

congregation in obedience to Holy Scripture and in response to the needs of the local community and the world. BCO I.2.1&2

4. *Priorities:* **Prayer and Making Disciples** *(equipping of the body for works of service /Eph. 4:11-13)*

5. *Agenda Focus:* A primary emphasis on Discipleship, Equipping in the Consistory's Role, and Prayer seeking to address only those items that cannot be handled by an empowered (delegated Authority & Responsibility) Board, Staff or Ministry team. This means = "Only the big stuff!"

6. *Specific Responsibilities:* Annual Report/Constitutional Inquiry (February), Nomination & Election Process (September), Annual Budget (October), Conduct Annual Meeting (November)

Focus of the Board of Elders

1. *Facilitated by:* **Vice President (Head Elder)**

2. *Role Summary:* Spiritual Oversight of Membership, Means of Grace {Worship & Sacraments}, and Ministry

3. *Book of Church Order Summary:* The board of elders shall be guided in its supervision of the membership of the church. At each regular meeting, the board of elders shall seek to determine whether any members of the congregation are in need of special care regarding their spiritual condition and/or are not making faithful use of the means of grace. The board of elders shall exercise Christian discipline with respect to any who continue in sin without repentance.

4. *Priorities:* **Prayer, Care, and Making Disciples** *(equipping of the body for works of service /Eph. 4:11-13)*

5. *Agenda Focus:* Defined Mission Priorities (gathered **Worship, Discipleship,** Missions & Service, and Stewardship) and the Empowerment & Encouragement of Ministry Teams under their oversight so that they are enabled to do "ministry" consistent with the Vision & Mission of Faith Community Church.

6. *Specific Responsibilities:* 1) Discipleship (UP, IN & OUT Focus – providing oversight to discipleship *vehicles* of **Small Groups and Missional Communities** to help people grow UP as a disciple and grow deep IN relationships with others as they engage in Living Faith OUT), 2) **Worship** (including Sacraments) (UP, IN, and OUT Focus – *inviting* disciples to grow UP & IN through the *vehicle* of gathered Worship as they grow in their *COVENANT* relationship with God and are *challenged* to engage in their *KINGDOM* responsibility by actively Living Faith OUT), 3) **Membership Oversight & Care** (IN Focus - New & Existing Members, Care, and Spiritual Discipline), as well as oversight of other partner ministries of the church (i.e.: Healing Rooms, Gap Ministries, Counseling, Boy Scouts, etc.)

7. *Elder Roles:* Seeking to maximize God's giftedness, the Elder roles will be differentiated as follows:

   a. *Administrative Elders* – Under the facilitation of the Senior Pastor and/or VP of Consistory and will have specific oversight of 1) Discipleship and 2) Worship Oversight

   b. *Shepherd/Care Elders* – Under the facilitation of the Pastor of Adult Discipleship & Care Equipping will include current elders as well as Great Consistory Elders as identified and charged with the specific oversight of 3) Membership Oversight & Care

Focus of the Board of Deacons

1. *Facilitated by:* **Chairperson of the Deacons**

2. *Role Summary:* Care that <u>M</u>eets needs, <u>I</u>s concerned with the redemption of hu<u>M</u>ankind, and enables <u>M</u>aterial Ministry

3. *Book of Church Order Summary:* The board of deacons shall serve those in distress and need. The deacons shall minister to the sick, the poor, the hurt, and the helpless, shall aid the victims of the world's abuse, and shall express the social concerns of the church. They shall oversee and carry out their work as those concerned with the redemption of humankind. Their focus is turned toward service and ministry both to the world and in the church. BCO I.6.2

4. *Priorities:* **Prayer, Care, and Making Disciples** *(equipping of the body for works of service /Eph. 4:11-13)*

5. *Agenda Focus:* Defined Mission Priorities (gathered Worship, Discipleship, **Missions & Service, and Stewardship**) and the Empowerment & Encouragement of Ministry Teams under their oversight so that they are enabled to do "ministry" consistent with the Vision & Mission of Faith Community Church.

6. *Specific Responsibilities:* **Missions & Service** (OUT Focus – developing relationships with partner ministries who engage in wholistic (non-enabling) ministry & provide opportunities for hands-on disciple engagement in Living Faith OUT in our *Jerusalem, Judea & Samaria, to the ends of the Earth*), **Benevolence** (IN Focus – providing financial assistance in our Jerusalem), **Connection & Stewardship** (UP, IN & OUT Focus - Welcoming & Connecting visitors & disciples, Identifying gifts, Equipping, and Assisting disciples as they engage in Living Faith OUT through their Time/Talent/Treasure), **Property &**

Grounds, and **Budget** (meeting as needed to develop/assess budget in meeting FCC Mission & Vision)

Focus of the Directional Board (Executive Team)

1. *Facilitated by:* **Vice President of the Board**

2. *Role Summary:* This group (predominantly comprised of the Officers of the church with select others of the Consistory) meets as needed when called by the VP to provide Mission & Vision direction to maximize the effectiveness of the Consistory and Boards in fulfilling the Missions & Vision.

3. *Priorities:* **Visionary focus for the Consistory & Boards and for Personnel**

4. *Agenda Focus:* This group's role is to consider any items deemed relevant to the fulfillment of the Mission & Vision of Faith Community Church and then to recommend or refer them to the Consistory or boards as deemed appropriate.

5. *Specific Responsibilities:* Authority & Responsibility is delegated to this group in Personnel & Human Resources as well as consideration of items relevant to fulfilling the Mission & Vision of the church.

Board Membership Expectations

1. *Be an Active Participant of the Board:*

    a. Make <u>attendance and participation</u> at all gatherings of the Consistory a priority, and inform the Senior Pastor of those gatherings that cannot be attended.

- **This includes active participation in all denomination and church provided Discipleship & Leadership Development events. As leaders, each Board & Staff member must be proactive in their growth and lead by their example as a disciple of Jesus Christ.**

b. Actively and honestly <u>share your Discernment</u> on all items considered, openly discussing your feelings and options regarding the subject at hand, while respecting the discernment and perspective of those around you in Christian love.

c. Always be prepared to <u>humble yourself,</u> recognizing that while we may not always agree, that our Aim is the Will of God … nothing more … nothing less … nothing else!

d. Recognizing that while we may not always be unanimous in our discernment, that after having shared our insights, findings, and feelings within the "confidence" of the Consistory, that we will <u>affirm the discernment of Consistory</u> to the congregation.

e. Sign and be a living example through an annual ***Accountability Covenant:***

Discipleship Covenant

I commit myself to participating in the life and ministry of Faith Community Church. In humility before God and with other disciples at Faith Community Church, I pledge myself as a developing disciple, seeking to grow in the Character & Competencies of Jesus Christ, to:

✓ Seek to interact with God continuously in <u>prayer</u> …

✓ Make it a priority to engage in gathered <u>worship</u> in this place …

✓ Be actively engaged in a <u>community</u> (Small Group or Missional Community) of Christian disciples in order that together we may <u>welcome</u> one another, <u>know</u> one another, <u>care</u> for one another, <u>pray</u> for one another, <u>support</u> one another, and <u>encourage</u> one another as we are being <u>transformed</u> by the Holy Spirit through the "rushing waters of the Word of God," more fully into the Character & Competencies of Jesus Christ …

✓ Strive to be a <u>living example</u> of the gospel, seeking to reveal the Character & Competencies of Jesus Christ in the world, and a model of stewardship through my returning of God's given time, talent, and treasure in my daily life …

✓ Look for opportunities to <u>"share my story"</u> of God's blessing, love, and un-merited grace for me in the person of Jesus Christ …

✓ Make <u>attendance and participation</u> at all Consistory gatherings and leadership development events a priority in my schedule …

✓ Being a role model of <u>"oversight & encouragement"</u> to the staff and ministry team identified, as they are the primary ones who lead from a position of empowered authority in their area of ministry …

APPENDIX 3
Board Equipping Workshop

Conducted annually with new board members in January, February, and March

Agenda Topics

THE *"WHAT"* OF THE BOARD:

- Previous Reading

    - A Forward View of the Board (provided above, in brief)

    - Authority & Responsibility Structures (organization chart)

- Session 1 - Role & Responsibilities

- Session 2 - Authority, Responsibility, and the Representative Principle

- Session 3 – Mission, Vision, and Core Values

THE *"HOW"* OF THE BOARD:

- Session 1 - Confidentiality

- Session 2 – Conflict & Systemic Thinking

- Session 3 – Discipleship Accountability

- Session 4 – Prayer, Spiritual Discernment, & Decision Making

    ○ Definition, Assumptions, and Notes

THE PRAYER, ACCOUNTABILITY, AND ENCOURAGEMENT FOCUS OF THE BOARD

- Casting of "Lots" for Elder/Deacon Prayer Partners during the coming year – Role:

    ○ Consistory Prayer Partners throughout the year

    ○ Sharing of Elder/Deacon Accountability Covenant (see "How" #3 above)

THE "WHAT" OF THE BOARD
Session 1 –Board Roles & Responsibilities

Preamble from the Book of Church Order (BCO) of the
Reformed Church in America

The purpose of the Reformed Church in America, together with all other churches of Christ, is <u>to minister to the total life of all people by preaching, teaching, and proclamation of the gospel of Jesus Christ, the Son of God, and by all Christian good works.</u> That purpose is achieved most effectively when good order and proper discipline are maintained by means of certain offices, governmental agencies, and theological and liturgical standards. <u>The Holy Scriptures are the only rule of faith and practice</u> in the Reformed Church in America. Its **Constitution** consists of the Doctrinal Standards (which are the *Belgic Confession of Faith*, the *Heidelberg Catechism* with its *Compendium*, the *Canons of the Synod of Dort*, and *The Belhar Confession*), the *Liturgy* with the *Directory for Worship*, the *Government of the Reformed Church in America*, and the *Disciplinary Procedures*.

Three offices are employed in the governmental functions of the Reformed Church, namely, *the minister of Word and sacrament* (hereinafter referred to as "minister"), the *elder*, and the *deacon*.

The governmental functioning of these offices takes place, not apart from, but in <u>harmony with the understanding of the mission of the church</u> and the nature of its ministry. This basic affirmation has three consequences.

- First, the purpose of church government is to aid the church in the development of its own life, in order that it may **carry out the mission of its Head**—to announce the good news of his Savior hood and extend his Lordship throughout the world.

- Second, **there is only one ministry and that ministry is shared by all Christians.** The particular ministries of those who hold office arise out of this common ministry in order to serve it.

- Third, the ecclesiastical offices which the Reformed Church deems necessary for its ordering are understood to be essentially functional in nature, and the term **"office" is everywhere viewed in terms of service.**

A Summary of the BCO (Part I) around the roles of the Board

Responsibilities of the Board

1. "Act in all matters calling for judgment and decision <u>which are not specifically assigned</u> to the board of elders or the board of deacons."

2. Shall provide a minister, or ministers, for the church.

3. "Provide services of <u>worship</u> and other activities and organizations in the church's life for the spiritual benefit and growth of Christ's people." - BCO lists requirements for "worship."

4. Make provisions for private administration of the <u>sacraments</u> in times of sickness or emergency.

5. Care and supervision of the church's property and financial interests.

6. Supervise <u>Elections</u> and assure rules of BCO are followed for elections.

7. "President and clerk shall <u>keep a careful register</u> of all baptisms and marriages, of all admissions to confessing membership, of all dismissions to other churches, and of the death of members."

8. Make a <u>statistical report</u> to Classis each year.

Officers of the Board

1. <u>President:</u> An Ordained pastor. "It shall be the duty of the president to state and explain the business to be transacted, to enforce the rules of order, and, in general, to maintain the decorum and dignity belonging to the church of Jesus Christ."

2. <u>Vice-president:</u> An elder.

3. <u>Secretary/Clerk:</u> Anyone "…whose duty shall be to keep a faithful record of all the proceedings of that body, and to furnish official notices in writing to all persons directly affected by decisions of the assembly."

Board of Elders – *in brief*

1. Supervise the membership of the church, considering if any members are in need of special care regarding their spiritual condition and/or are not making faithful use of means of grace . . .

2. "The board of elders shall exercise Christian discipline with respect to any who continue in sin without repentance."

Board of Deacons – *in brief*

1. "The board of deacons shall serve those in distress and need. The deacons shall minister to the sick, the poor, the hurt, and the helpless, shall aid the victims of the world's abuse, and shall express the social concerns of the church. They shall oversee and carry out their work as those concerned with the redemption of humankind. Their focus is turned toward service and ministry both to the world and in the church."

2. The board of deacons … shall render an account in Consistory of its ministry, including its collection and distribution of the benevolence contributions of the congregation."

Transaction of Business

1. Elders and deacons have equal voice.

2. A quorum = a majority of the Consistory members regularly convened.

3. All meetings begin and end in prayer.

4. A member of the consistory shall not have the right to protest any act or decision of that body, but shall have the right to redress by appeal or complaint to the classis. See 1.I.4.4 for specific details re: votes.

5. May invite another pastor or Classis representative to preside over meetings.

6. A meeting shall happen if requested by three members of Consistory.

7. Consistory shall submit minutes of its meetings to the Classis whenever they ask for it.

THE "WHAT" OF THE BOARD
Session 2 – Authority, Responsibility, and the Representative Principle

BCO (Preamble)

The Head of the Church. The Reformed churches confess that <u>Jesus Christ is the only Head of his church</u>. The Scriptures call the church his body, and our Lord the Head of that body. He is therefore in the closest and most vital relationship to his church. As the church's true Head, he has complete authority over its life, and therefore the church must ever yield to him a ready obedience and faithfulness.

The Nature of the Church's Authority. All authority exercised in the church is received from Christ, the only Head of the church. <u>The authority exercised by those holding office in the church is delegated authority</u>. Their appointment to their special tasks is by the Spirit of the Lord, and they are responsible first of all to the Lord of the church. The Spiritual authority given to office-holders is exercised in the assemblies of the church. The offices meeting together represent the fullness of Christ's ministry. <u>No office functions apart from the other offices</u>. Reformed governance understands that the <u>greater assemblies care for the ministry that extends beyond the purview of the lesser assemblies without infringing upon the responsibilities of the lesser</u>. Consistories, classes, and synods work together in mission and ministry within their shared boundaries.

The Representative Principle. The power which Jesus Christ bestows upon his church is <u>mediated by the Holy Spirit to all the people</u>. Since not everyone in the church can hold an office, and since the offices differ among themselves in function, some persons will always be subject, within the proper exercise of authority, to the decisions of others. Since the whole church cannot meet together at one time and place to deliberate, representative governing bodies must be established on the various levels. <u>The unity of the church is preserved in acceptance of the</u>

fact that all are governed by the decisions made in their behalf by those who represent them.

Government by Elders. The Reformed churches have sought to follow the practice of the churches whose experience is recorded in the New Testament. The churches then were ruled by "presbyters" or "elders," just as the synagogues from which the first Christian converts came were ruled by elders. The Reformed churches consider the minister to be an elder of a special kind, called in some churches of the Reformed order, the "teaching elder." Ministers and elders therefore govern the church together.

THE "WHAT" OF CONSISTORY
Session 3 – Mission, Vision, and Values of Faith Community Church

In a *Forward View of the Board*, we discussed that the role of the board could best be summarized as:

Discerning, Discussing, and Enabling the "Will of God" to become a reality at Faith Community Church ...

As we seek discernment and consider specific opportunities to "do" ministry, it is easy to become distracted and "caught up" in the tactical elements of a specific ministry or in the passions of one or a few individuals.

In recognition of this human tendency toward "details", <u>the Board (the "called" leadership) must always keep its focus on the "Bigger Picture" of the Mission, Vision, and Values of Christ's church in this place.</u>

Mission: *Making Disciples of Jesus Christ who are Growing UP, IN, and OUT - No Excuses!*

Vision: *Cultivating Missional Communities of unleashed disciples ushering in the Kingdom of God.*

Values:

In making disciples of Jesus Christ, we place a high value on F.A.I.T.H.

- **F**ruitful in mission and service - *making disciples of Jesus Christ who usher in God's kingdom, both locally and around the world*

- **A**ctively making disciples - *demonstrating the Character & Competencies of Jesus Christ*

- **I**nspiring in gathered worship - *praising God alone as we refine our*

157

hearts to those things that break the heart of God

- **T**heologically Sound - *teaching Truth from God's Word, affirming the witness of the church through the ages*

- **H**armonious in our service - *practicing the Truth of God's Word experiencing transformation as disciples of Jesus Christ (UP), as we live as a family on mission (IN), and as we serve as a sent people of God in the world (OUT)*

THE "HOW" OF THE BOARD
Session 1 – Confidentiality

Ministry Confidentiality Defined – being dedicated and committed to the mission of the church, and able to hold <u>in strict confidence</u> information related to <u>persons</u> and <u>issues</u> within the ministry of the church.

Situational Case Study:

- As you are approaching the doctor's office for your annual physical, you encounter a member of the congregation who is just leaving. After you exchange greetings and inform the member of your purpose for being at the doctor (annual physical), you ask the nature of her visit.

- The member shares that as a result of a previous visit, the doctor suggested running a few tests. The nurse called yesterday and asked her to come in today. The test results were not good and there is a suspicion of cancer and that more tests need to be run.

- In the course of your discussion, the member shares that both her mother and father had both died of cancer. She also shared that her husband had just lost his job, that finances were tight, and that they have been operating on a "Catastrophic Only" health insurance policy with a very high deductible.

- She is understandably scared ….

As a Board Member, how do you respond to the Member?

- *How can the church help? (Open ended)*

- *Can we share this News with the Pastors?*

- *Can we add this Information to the Prayer Line?*

- *Can we add this prayer request to the Bulletin?*

- *Can we contact the Deacons to consider Benevolence assistance?*

What do you say to others, even if she told you NO, please don't tell anyone?

- Do you call the church office or pastor "on call" because they should know?

- When you get home, do you tell your wife so that she can pray, too?

- When you get together that night with your close friends to play games, do you tell them so that just they can be praying for her and her family?

  - *Depending on their responses to your previous questions – Perhaps Nothing!*

  - *If they say No, or Not Now! You have to respect their wishes*

  - *But even if they Tell me No, can I share it with my spouse or the pastor? No! Confidentiality is Confidentiality!*

  - <u>*What if a few days later at church, somebody says to you – "Hey did you hear about Lori? She's got cancer you know." What do you do then?*</u>

    - *That is when you say nothing to the individual who brought it to your attention*

    - *Go back to the Member and say – Someone mentioned to me that they had heard about your cancer (Insuring clarity that you did not break the confidence)*

    - *Ask again if now is the time that the Church can help … in what way!*

THE "HOW" OF THE BOARD
Session 2 – Conflict & Systemic Thinking

Systemic Thinking Defined – a view about the universe (a picture of reality) that affirms that everything that exists is in an ongoing mutual relationship with every other reality.

Larry Graham

Situational Case Study:

- John and Sarah are extremely anxious about what just happened in the congregation. Somewhat unaware of their own anxiety, they <u>expect</u> the leadership of the church to be anxious about and to address the situation.

- Since John and Sarah <u>cannot see themselves talking about this situation</u> with the Pastor, they instead talk about their disagreement with a few of their friends and then with members of the consistory.

- John and Sarah feel much better about their situation after they discuss it with the Consistory members. They now experience a sense of relief from their anxiety as <u>they now feel that their anxiety is being carried by others in the church leadership</u>. They quietly hope that their concern will be shared with the Pastor by others.

- The <u>Board members now feel burdened in their relationship both with John and Sarah … and with the Pastor</u>. They understand the un-communicated desires of John and Sarah for them to "deal with" the issue, but they also feel that this conflict is not theirs and will bring conflict into their relationship with Pastor Jill.

161

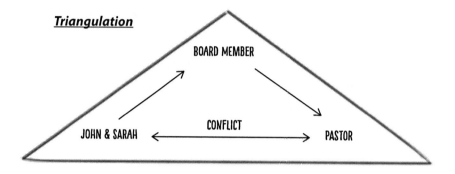

Triangulation

BOARD MEMBER

JOHN & SARAH ←——— CONFLICT ———→ PASTOR

If this was a "personal conflict" between John & Sarah and the Pastor, as a board member, how would you respond to John and Sarah? You should say:

- *Have you spoken with the Pastor?*

- *Would you like me to arrange a visit between you and the Pastor?*

- *I would encourage you to arrange a visit and speak "face to face" with the Pastor.*

If this was a church related issue in which the Board had been involved in the decision, how would you respond to John and Sarah? Do you:

- … "pass the buck" to the Pastor and let this role deal with it?

- … convene an emergency meeting of the Board to communicate the "anxiety" in the congregation surrounding this issue?

- … share that while you can understand their concern, that this issue has been considered by the Board and that the direction of the pastor is consistent with the leadership of the church?

THE "HOW" OF THE BOARD
Session 3 – Discipleship Accountability

"If you put these instructions before the brothers and sisters,
you will be a good servant of Christ Jesus, nourished on the words of the faith
and of the sound teaching you have followed …
These are the things you must insist on and teach.
Let no one despise your youth, but <u>set the believers an example</u> in speech
and conduct, in love, in faith, in purity.
Until I arrive, give attention to the <u>public reading of scripture</u>, to exhorting,
to teaching. Do not neglect the gift that is in you, which was given to you
through the prophecy with the <u>laying on of hands</u> by the council of elders.
Put these things into practice, devote yourself to them, <u>so that all may see</u>
<u>your progress</u>.
I Timothy 4:6-15

In the spirit of Paul's letter to Timothy, each of us has been "called" into ministry and given the gift of the "laying on of hands".

While we acknowledge our sin and shortcomings, we also acknowledge our responsibility to be a "good servant of Jesus Christ." With Paul's charge to Timothy … and to us in mind, as members of the Consistory & Staff of the church, we hereby desire to set ourselves before the believers an "example in speech and conduct, in love, in faith, and in purity."

Board & Staff Accountability Covenant

I commit myself to participating in the life and ministry of Faith Community Church in the coming year. Before God and with the other members of the Faith Community Consistory & Staff, I pledge myself as a disciple of Jesus Christ, and commit myself to:

- ✓ Seek to interact with God continuously in prayer …

- ✓ Make it a priority to engage in gathered worship in this place …

- ✓ Be actively engaged in a community (Small Group or Missional Community) of Christian disciples in order that together we may welcome one another, know one another, care for one another, pray for one another, support one another, and encourage one another as we are being transformed by the Holy Spirit through the "rushing waters of the Word of God," more fully into the Character & Competencies of Jesus Christ …

- ✓ Strive to be a living example of the gospel, seeking to reveal the Character & Competencies of Jesus Christ in the world, and a model of stewardship through my returning of God's given time, talent, and treasure in my daily life …

- ✓ Look for opportunities to "share my story" of God's blessing, love, and un-merited grace for me in the person of Jesus Christ …

- ✓ Make attendance and participation at all Consistory gatherings and leadership development events a priority in my schedule …

- ✓ Being a role model of "oversight & encouragement" to the staff and ministry team identified, as they are the primary ones who lead from a position of empowered authority in their area of ministry …

Board or Staff Member: _____

Date:_____

THE "HOW" OF THE BOARD
Session 4 –Prayer, Spiritual Discernment, & Decision Making

Definition - What is Discernment?

- ✓ It is easier to speak of what something is not. Discernment is not a "silver bullet", a "magic pill", or a "litmus test" to be applied at key moments of decision-making in the life of the church.

- ✓ Discernment is precisely the Holy Spirit acting within us and is simply our awareness of that action. Discernment is experiencing with understanding and commitment the presence and guidance of God in one's whole life.

- ✓ According to St. Ignatius, "our first aim should be to seek to serve God." I am to keep my aim to the end for which I am created. That aim is "to Praise God ... and then to desire to be "indifferent" and willing to accept and follow whatever is to the greater glory of God!" What does it mean to be indifferent? To John of the Cross, it would have been translated as having a "detachment," but to people of our culture, the word indifferent might be better understood simply as having "biblical faith" or an openness to God. Indifference is simply a willingness to move in whatever direction God calls without putting limitations or boundaries of where that movement will take us.

- ✓ Therefore, the goal of discernment is not to find an answer (or the answer) to a given question. In fact, discernment doesn't even fit within the context of our outcome/objective driven mentality of culture or workplace. No, the goal of discernment is the (good) fruit of the spirit. For St. Ignatius this goal was consolation (love, peace, and joy). And if we are living in an environment that is discerning God's will, the Lord will be present & acting, the signs & fruits of God's presence will be there - whether joy in suffering, or peace in persecution.

- ✓ "Discernment can never be successfully carried out if it is only an occasional act that is foreign to ones usual total life." It must be ongoing and continual - A part of every activity of life and of the church. And if we seek to live in an environment in which "the Holy Spirit is active throughout the church", we must then recognize that "individuals and groups need to be able to distinguish the Spirit's music from other melodies that float upon the air."

✓ This is the heart of discernment in today's context of the church - A post-reformation context in which we are able to enter into the Holy of Holies and to hear God's voice without the aid of an intermediary. A context in which the church collectively listens in order to discern the loving desires of God's. In an environment where the discernment of God's voice is fostered in this way, the church will tend to reach different conclusions from those of logic, persuasion or everyday common sense. Logic, debate, persuasive argumentation and politics will be minimized and put aside as we listen and recognize the unique ways of God's leading, being accountable to live in faithful response. We will not be concerned about knowing the answer or the answer that is most acceptable to the majority – but only about knowing God's will.

Assumptions - What are my Assumptions for discernment in the church?

✓ **God's children:** I believe that those who have been adopted as children of God are in the midst of a lifelong process of transformation and desire to do God's will.

✓ **Activity of the Good Spirit upon God's children:** It is characteristic of God and his Angels, when they act upon the soul, to give true happiness and spiritual joy to banish all the sadness and disturbances which are caused by the enemy. (Ignatius, #329)

✓ **Activity of the Evil Spirit God's upon God's children:** I believe that it is characteristic of the evil spirit to harass with anxiety, to afflict with sadness, to raise obstacles backed by fallacious reasoning that disturb the soul (Ignatius, #315). Further, that the evil spirit is deceptive and can assume the appearance of angels of light … he will suggest holy and pious thoughts that are wholly in conformity with the sanctity of the soul and then afterward, he will endeavor little by little to end by drawing the soul into hidden snares and designs. (Ignatius, #332)

✓ **World and Western Culture:** I believe that we must clearly recognize we live in a fallen world and in a culture plagued with excessive individualism. Even though God desires true happiness and spiritual joy for us, this can only be accomplished with spiritual discernment in which we "allow God's received revelation to set the agenda for our choices." To live in an environment of spiritual discernment, we must be willing to challenge the accepted values of our culture and society (Lonsdale, pg. 36)

✓ **Our Help is in the name of the Lord:** I believe that with our acknowledgment of the presence of evil in the world and in our culture, we must firmly state as a community of faith that "our help is in the name of the Lord, who made Heaven and Earth." A critical element in fostering an environment of discernment is recognizing that it is <u>not a skill to for man to develop, but a reliance on GOD and an active seeking and waiting for God's leading</u> (Dougherty, pg. 26). In this reliance, we (individuals and groups) must check both ourselves and our culture at the door in order to hear God's voice.

✓ **How we hear God speak:** I believe that God speaks to us today as he did in days of old. I believe that God speaks to us if we listen through Prayer, the Holy Bible, through the Discerning Voices of the Church, and through Circumstance. And I believe that God most often speaks through these channels in a "still, small voice" that our culture of "doing" does not easily hear. As a result, in order to hear God's voice, periods of silence and intentional quiet need to be placed at a priority in the life of the church and its leaders. Times in which we are intentionally open to the Presence of God, in which we are willing to: (Dougherty, pg. 80)

   ○ Be <u>present</u> … without an agenda

   ○ <u>Resist</u> the temptation to take control … to seek an "outcome"

   ○ <u>Pray</u> for "space" … to be aware of God's Presence and hear his voice

Community Discernment in the church?

For significant items of discernment, Charles Olsen and Danny Morris (in part based on the work of St. Ignatius) have developed a process of 10 stepping stones of discernment (Olsen, pg. 78-79). These 10 stepping stones include:

1. **Framing** – Identifies the focus for the discernment of God's will. In short, what is the question to be discerned?

2. **Grounding** – What are the guiding principles, values, beliefs we must consider? In short, what are our boundaries for discernment?

3. **Shedding** – What must I be willing to lay aside before I can proceed with discernment, or before I am willing to accept the outcome of God's discernment over my own? I believe this is perhaps the most important stepping stone for effective discernment in our culture.

4. **Rooting** – What are the traditions, stories, themes and images within the situation at hand? The telling of these traditions and stories may confront, confirm, or even transform the direction of the discernment.

5. **Listening** – Periods of silence and prolonged periods of prayer are needed in order to cut through the clutter in order to hear the direction of the Holy Spirit. Also we need to listen to each other and the voices of the discerning community of faith around us.

6. **Exploring** – This is permission for us to freely explore and let our playful imaginations consider options and paths that lie within the guiding principle in which we are grounded.

Subject: Invitation: Small church BIG MISSION NETWORK gathering @ Mon Apr 30, 2018 9am - 10am (PDT) (Ken Winter)

From: Jeffrey Allen <jeffreyallen63@gmail.com>

Date: 4/29/2018 7:02 AM

To: kwinter@ssctv.net, Steve DeLisle <sdelisle48@gmail.com>, William Coker Jr <rewwbcjr@gmail.com>, Roger Grandia <rogergrandia@gmail.com>, tmabie@verizon.net, Chael Tiller <chaeltiller@gmail.com>, seth sundstrom <sethsundstrom@gmail.com>, pastoral@ptd.net

---

Jeffrey Allen has invited you to Small church BIG MISSION NETWORK gathering

Title:	Small church BIG MISSION NETWORK gathering
Location:	https://zoom.us/j/3658030640
When:	Monday, April 30, 2018 9:00 AM – 10:00 AM
Organizer:	Jeffrey Allen <jeffreyallen63@gmail.com>

Description:	Greetings Small church BIG MISSION practitioners,
	
	I am inviting you to join me tomorrow morning at 10am Mountain time for an introductory session of the Small church on a BIG Mission online Network.
	
	In the session tomorrow, I will share briefly about the purpose of this network and then share about the parable of the soils and consider the application of the 8/6/4 principle in the context of smaller churches.
	
	I hope you will be able to join me.
	
	Jeff Allen is inviting you to a scheduled Zoom meeting.
	
	Join from PC, Mac, Linux, iOS or Android: <a href="https://www.google.com/url?q=https%3A%2F%2F zoom.us%2Fj%2F3658030640&sa=D& usg=AFQjCNG72yQUBedBK9TCBbJNzkdWRCm9NA" target="_blank">https://zoom.us/j/3658030640</a>
	
	Or iPhone one-tap :
	   US: +16468769923,,3658030640# or +16699006833,,3658030640#
	
	Or Telephone:
	   Dial(for higher quality, dial a number based on your current location):
	     US: +1 646 876 9923 or +1 669 900 6833 or +1 408 638 0968
	     Meeting ID: 365 803 0640
	   International numbers available: <a href="https://www.google.com/url?q=https%3A%2F%2Fzoom.us%2Fu%2FlYbK9&sa=D&usg=AFQjCNE_1- LeY4VTr1p0WU9G3zYndbSxAw" target="_blank">https://zoom.us/u/lYbK9</a>

:.:.:

Please do not edit this section of the description.

This event has a Google Hangouts video call.
Join: https://hangouts.google.com/hangouts/_/calendar /amVmZnJleWFsbGVuNjNAZ21haWwuY29t.2bmof2eip81k537f2ucvq4tcio?hs=121

View your event at https://www.google.com/calendar/event?action=VIEW& eid=MmJtb2YyZWlwODFrNTM3ZjJ1Y3ZxNHRjaW8ga3dpbnRlckBzc2N0di5uZXQQ& tok=MjQjamVmZnJleWFsbGVuNjNAZ21haWwuY29tMTU0MmMwYThhZTU0M2NmYzY3NzQ3MzBiN2Y0MiRhOWFiNTE0ZWZjMQ& ctz=America%2FLos_Angeles&hl=en&es=1.

:.:.:

Attendees:

Steve DeLisle <sdelisle48@gmail.com>
William Coker Jr <rewwbcjr@gmail.com>
Roger Grandia <rogergrandia@gmail.com>
tmabie@verizon.net <tmabie@verizon.net>
Chael Tiller <chaeltiller@gmail.com>
Ken Winter <kwinter@ssctv.net>
Jeffrey Allen <jeffreyallen63@gmail.com>
seth sundstrom <sethsundstrom@gmail.com>
pastoral@ptd.net <pastoral@ptd.net>

---Attachments:---

invite.ics   4.1 KB

7. **Improving** – This works in consultation and prayer to improve each option under consideration until it becomes the best that we can imagine it to be within the yearning of God.

8. **Weighing** – Utilizing our intellect to sort and test the options or paths in response to the leading of God's spirit.

9. **Closing** – This is the stepping stone which brings the explorations to a conclusion, moving toward the selection of an option which is given weight by the Spirit of God.

10. **Resting** – This tests the decision by allowing it to rest near our hearts to determine whether it brings primarily feelings of consolation or desolation.

ENDNOTES

1. Small business (zero employees = 78% and up to 500 employees = 99%) amount to 99 percent of businesses in the United States. http://smallbusiness. chron.com/percentage-small-large-businesses-america-59860.html

According to the Hartford Institute for Religion. The median church in the United States has 75 regular participants in Sunday worship. http://hirr. hartsem.edu/research/fastfacts/fast_facts.html#sizecong)

2. http://leadership.fuller.edu/Leadership/Resources/Part_4-Leading_for_ Transformative_Change/I__Technical_and_Adaptive_Change.aspx

CPSIA information can be obtained
at www.ICGtesting.com
Printed in the USA
FFOW03n0354111217
43921216-42976FF